PRINCE ALBERT
AND THE VICTORIAN AGE

Prince Albert as Chancellor of the
University of Cambridge

PRINCE ALBERT
AND THE
VICTORIAN AGE

A SEMINAR HELD IN MAY 1980 IN
COBURG UNDER THE AUSPICES OF
THE UNIVERSITY OF BAYREUTH
AND THE CITY OF COBURG

EDITED BY
JOHN A. S. PHILLIPS

CAMBRIDGE UNIVERSITY PRESS

CAMBRIDGE
LONDON NEW YORK NEW ROCHELLE
MELBOURNE SYDNEY

Published by the Press Syndicate of the University of Cambridge
The Pitt Building, Trumpington Street, Cambridge CB2 1RP
32 East 57th Street, New York, NY 10022, USA
296 Beaconsfield Parade, Middle Park, Melbourne 3206, Australia

The illustrations are taken from the Royal Collection at Windsor Castle
and are reproduced with the gracious permission of H.M. The Queen.

First published 1981

Printed in Great Britain
at the University Press, Cambridge

British Library Cataloguing in Publication Data
Prince Albert and the Victorian age.
1. Albert, *Prince, consort of Victoria, Queen
of Great Britain*
I. Phillips, John
941.081   DA551
ISBN 0 521 24242 8

CONTENTS

ILLUSTRATIONS

Prince Albert as Chancellor of the University of Cambridge
frontispiece

In the chapter by Sir Robin Mackworth-Young:

Message from
His Majesty King Baudouin,
King of the Belgians

ON THE MEMORABLE AND SCHOLARLY OCCASION of a seminar (held by the University of Bayreuth and the City of Coburg) devoted to 'Prince Albert and the Victorian Age', under the Patronage of His Royal Highness The Prince Philip, Duke of Edinburgh, represented by His Royal Highness The Duke of Gloucester, I send greetings to the Patron, his Representative, the University of Bayreuth, the City of Coburg and to all those attending and assisting in the organisation of the seminar. In particular I acknowledge the contribution which has been made to the seminar by the President of the University of Bayreuth, the Lord Mayor and citizens of Coburg together with the Chairman of the Coburg Rural District Council, as well as national and municipal bodies, not forgetting those citizens who have opened their houses to visitors from abroad for the duration of the seminar.

Prince Albert of Sachsen-Coburg-Gotha, Consort of Queen Victoria, was the nephew of King Léopold I, the founder of the Belgian dynasty. Without ever wearing a crown The Prince Consort represented in his life and work the finest qualities of modern, constitutional kingship. I salute his memory and the country and place of his birth – Coburg and Rosenau.

I wish the seminar devoted to establishing the importance of Prince Albert in the Victorian Age every success and await with interest report of its deliberations which I am sure will further Anglo-German-Belgian friendship based upon a new and objective study of history.

BAUDOUIN

Message from
H.R.H. The Prince Philip,
Duke of Edinburgh

PRINCE ALBERT was a man of many talents and wide interests, who exerted a very considerable influence on the whole character of the Victorian age. I am delighted that his home town of Coburg and the University of Bayreuth have organised this Seminar in which so many distinguished scholars from his own and from his adopted country have agreed to participate. I am sure it is just the sort of project that would have given Prince Albert great pleasure.

Among many other things, I hope the Seminar will encourage interest both in the preservation and in the practical use of Schloss Rosenau. Throughout his life his beloved birthplace was never far from his thoughts and while it exists it will be a constant reminder of his influence and achievements.

PHILIP

EDITOR'S PREFACE

IT WAS His Royal Highness The Prince Philip who first suggested converting Rosenau Castle, Prince Albert's birthplace so cherished by Queen Victoria, into an Anglo-German venue combined with a Prince Albert archive. Yet the castle, used as an old people's home after the war, needed extensive restoration which was difficult to finance. The Bavarian State has already rescued the castle park from the undergrowth and carried out costly repairs to the roof, but it is unlikely that the full restoration will be completed until 1985.

With the holding of a seminar it was intended to revive interest in Rosenau. There were times when it seemed that the castle would never be restored and to this day the interior presents the visitor with a depressing sight: formerly beautifully proportioned rooms are still crudely partitioned off into cubicles covered over with wallpaper once antiseptically white, now less so, cracked and peeling. In places one can still see signs of the original decoration peeping through ugly coats of distemper.

The seminar on 'Prince Albert and the Victorian Age' was held by the University of Bayreuth and the City of Coburg on 22–3 May 1980 in the imposing Ehrenburg Palace, Coburg. His Majesty King Baudouin of the Belgians graciously sent a Message, as did H.R.H. The Prince Philip, Patron of the seminar, who was represented by H.R.H. The Duke of Gloucester. This volume of the seminar proceedings is a record of that scholarly and memorable occasion.

On Saturday, 7 March the inauguration took place of the Prince Albert Society, founded to foster Anglo-German research into the Victorian Age. Re-examining history may perhaps remove some of the misunderstandings about Anglo-German relations in the past and thus lead to better mutual understanding in the future. The University of Bayreuth is also planning to establish an Institute for Victorian Studies. Perhaps both institute and society may find a home in the Rosenau.

All these plans are but expressions of the desire to further Anglo-German friendship in the spirit of Prince Albert whose untimely death, followed tragically by that of his son-in-law, the Kaiser Friedrich III, had the consequences touched upon by several of the speakers at the seminar.

As editor of the Proceedings I wish to record my gratitude to Her Majesty The Queen for gracious permission to reproduce the illustrations to Sir Robin Mackworth-Young's lecture. I am also most grateful to Professor Owen Chadwick, Regius Professor of Modern History in the University of Cambridge, who represented the Vice-Chancellor of Cambridge University at the seminar and, at very short notice, kindly wrote the introduction to this book and thus enriched it.

J.A.S.P.

March 1981

ACKNOWLEDGEMENTS

THE University of Bayreuth and the City of Coburg wish to thank the following people for their support and invaluable help in connection with the Prince Albert Seminar:

Der Ministerpräsident des Freistaats Bayern Dr h. c. Franz Josef Strauß

Herr Staatsminister Dr Karl Hillermeier

H.R.H. Princess Margaret of Hesse and the Rhine

Hans Heinrich Freiherr Herwarth von Bittenfeld

His Excellency Sir Oliver Wright, G.C.M.G., G.C.V.O., D.S.C., formerly Her Majesty's Ambassador to the Federal Republic of Germany

S. G. Eldon, Esq., Second Secretary, British Embassy, Bonn

Adrian H. Reed, Esq., formerly H.M. Consul-General, Munich

Alex Mineeff, Esq., O.B.E., Vice-Consul, Munich

David Rundle, Esq., Regional Director, British Council, Munich

Monsieur A. De Buck, Cultural Attaché, Belgian Embassy, Cologne

S.E., I.H. Graf und Gräfin zu Ortenburg, Tambach

Sebastian Freiherr von Rotenhahn, Rentweinsdorf

Eyring Freiherr von Rotenhahn, Eyrichshof

†Wolfram Freiherr von Erffa, Ahorn

Frau Uta Benecke, Berghof, Trieb

Frau Sybille Preuschen, Ziegelsdorf

Herr Dr jur. Klaus Groebe, Landrat a. D. und Frau Elisabet Groebe, Coburg

Miss Hermione Hobhouse, Secretary: the Victorian Society

Bayreuth University: Herr Professor Dr Erwin Herrmann, Herr Dr Karl-Friedrich Kühner, Herr Dr Oswald Stille, Dr Eckhard Lieb, Herr Amtmann Christian Bär, Frau Erika Duncanson, Frau Fleming, Frau Angela Morales, Frau Elke Ott, Herr Ottmar Foerster, Herr Hermann Eschenbacher, Frl. Regina Kattwinkel, Herr Hans Eller, Herr Michael Neuer, David Barron, Esq., Miss Cheryl David, Miss Brigitte Gruber. *Bayreuth:* Albrecht Graf von und zu Egloffstein, Herr Dpl. Kfm. Wolfgang Berlinghof. *Brussels:* Monsieur Herman Liebaers, Grand Maréchal de la Cour, Monsieur Jean-Pierre Dutry. *Coburg:* Herr Herbert Appeltshauser;

Acknowledgements

Herr Dr Harold Bachmann, 1. Vorsitzender Historischer Verein Coburg e. V.; Herr Bibl. Dir. Dr Jürgen Erdmann; Herr Rüdiger Feiler, 1. Vorsitzender des Aero-Club; Herr Regierungsamtsrat Konrad Festnacht; Herr Hans Fiedler und Frau Heidemarie Fiedler (Max Fiedler); Herr Bürgermeister Ferdinand Fischer; Frau Elisabeth Geelhaar; Herr Götz, E.P.H.K., Landespolizei; Herr Eduard Haerter; Frau Dagmar Heß; Herr Detlef Höhn, Verkehrsamt; Frau Ruth Hornung; Herr Helmut Judex Kilian, P.K. i. B.G.S.; Herr Intendant Dr Tebbe H. Kleen; Herr Landrat Helmut Knauer; Herr Museumsdirektor Dr Joachim Kruse; Herr Alfred Maier, P.H.K., Landespolizei; Herr Regierungsamtmann Mattstedt, Coburger Landesstiftung; Herr Technischer Amtmann Wolfgang Nahr, Landbauamt; Herr Erich Oberender, Staatsarchiv; Herr Verkehrsdirektor Klaus Paskuda; Frau Eveline Rosensprung; Herr Verwaltungsdirektor Erich Sauerbrei; Herr Gerhard Schreier; Hans-Georg Schneider; Herr Bauoberrat Hermann Stamm; Herr Ottmar Stöcker, Ltd. P.D. i B.G.S.; Dr Klaus Freiherr Andrian von Wehrburg, Staatsarchiv; Hotel Goldener Anker, Hotel Goldene Traube & Hotel Schloß Neuhof. *Munich:* Hans Jürgen Freiherr von Crailsheim, Präsident der B.V.; Herr Dr Lorenz Seelig; Herr Veit, Bayer. Verwaltung der Staatl. Schlösser, Gärten und Seen; Herr Ministerial-dirigent Dr Joseph Huber; Alexander Freiherr von Hornstein; Herr Dr Erwin Arnold, Bayer. Staatsbibliothek; Desmond Clayton, Esq., Bayer. Fernsehen. *Nürnberg:* Herr Dr Manfred Boos, Bayer. Rundfunk. *Friedrich-Alexander-Universität Erlangen-Nürnberg:* Frau Professor Dr Gertrud Walter; Herr Professor Dr Erwin Wolff. *Universität Regensburg:* Herr Dr Werner Arens. *Windsor Castle:* The Hon. Mrs Jane Roberts, Curator of the Print Room; Miss Jane Langton, M.V.O., Registrar. Dr Max and Mrs Michaelis, Rycote Park, England; Mrs Jackie Toop, Cape Town, South Africa; Corporal Trench, the Gloucestershire Regiment.

The University of Bayreuth and the City of Coburg wish to acknowledge the assistance of the following institutions: Bayerische Staatskanzlei, Belgische Botschaft – Kulturabteilung, Deutscher Akademische Austauschdienst, Ministry of Defence, British Army of the Rhine, the Gloucestershire Regiment, the Victorian Society.

The editor of these Proceedings also wishes to thank The Rt. Hon. Sir Keith Joseph, Bt, M.P., Lt. Col. S.C.M. Bland, C.V.O. and R.H. Davies, Esq., C.B.E.

INTRODUCTION: PRINCE ALBERT AS CHANCELLOR OF THE UNIVERSITY OF CAMBRIDGE

OWEN CHADWICK

THIS BOOK came out of the seminar at Coburg, hospitably organised under the auspices of the University of Bayreuth and the City of Coburg.

No history is better than history recreated at the place where the events happened. The meeting at Coburg on 22–3 May 1980 was just such an experience. The participants could look out of a window and see what Queen Victoria saw when she visited the town. They could breathe the atmosphere of the old princely city, an atmosphere without which Prince Albert is hardly intelligible, and which deepens the understanding of Queen Victoria. They could hear of the difficulties and friendships between Prince Albert and a succession of British Prime Ministers, and have a chance of realising what it must have felt like, coming from the quiet beauty of Coburg to the smoke and public duties of early Victorian London. The meeting gave a chance for British and German historians, interested in cognate problems of the mid-nineteenth century, to hear each other's views and discuss them. In addition, the visit of the seminar to Prince Albert's birthplace at Schloss Rosenau gave a new impetus to an older plan to restore Rosenau, an enchanting house in an enchanting park, and perhaps to use it as a centre for British–German studies.

British universities in the early Victorian age needed some of the insights which German universities could have brought them. In philosophy and history, in classics and philology, Germany was pre-eminent. The university system, built by the Enlightenment on an older Protestant basis, had proved its worth. A few (but very few) Englishmen tried to make the British understand what could be found in Germany, and even to know something of Goethe and Schiller. Only the music of Germany had domiciled itself in Britain. In every other field of culture the relations of the two countries were infertile. The cultural link is to this day less close than it should be. The city of Coburg stood as the symbol of a meeting between the cultural ideals of Britain and Germany, their modes of thought, study of history, concern for scientific truth, love of art and architecture, and even of an embryo international friendship which later events came near to destroying.

The Chancellor of the University of Cambridge, the Duke of Northumberland, died in February 1847. Since the days of the early Reformation the Chancellors of Oxford and Cambridge had had no real constitutional power inside their universities. The Vice-Chancellor exercised such power as those democratic societies of individualistic scholars allowed to their executive. The Chancellor, inside the university, became a figure-head. But the members of the university usually chose a man powerful in the world, who could protect them from the intrusions of radical politicians. And if he was powerful in the world, he had influence, and patronage, and leverage, which at times could make him powerful in the university. This the universities had started not to like. By the time that Queen Victoria came to the throne, the University of Cambridge had begun to prefer pleasant courteous aristocrats who would not have too much leverage even if they helped the members of the university by their patronage.

The Chancellor was unkind to die in February 1847. For at that moment the old universities of Britain, no longer the only two universities but still, for a few more years, the only universities which counted, were in political controversy. Under the widened franchise, and the new power of dissenters, and Irish Roman Catholics in Parliament, a lot of critics were vocal both inside and outside Parliament. These colleges were the only properly endowed places of higher education in the country; yet their advantages were available only to members of the Church of England, and their curriculum was so narrow that they were failing to teach most of the subjects which were important to the modern world. At Cambridge the only subjects to count towards the degree of Bachelor of Arts were classics and mathematics. The whole world of science, history, modern languages was a closed book to most of their graduates.

All this made one of Prince Albert's chances of serving the country into which he married and the field of one of his lasting achievements.

The members of the University of Cambridge who in February 1847 wanted him as Chancellor, wanted him for the wrong reasons. Prince Albert was deeply concerned over education. That meant nothing to them. They were hardly aware that he cared about the subject. They were frightened of politicians interfering with their ways. They fancied that it would be more difficult for politicians to interfere too drastically with an institution which had the Queen's husband at its head. They were afraid of the Liberal government of Lord John Russell appointing a commission to inquire into them. They thought it would be harder to appoint a commission of inquiry into a body which included Prince Albert. They had no notion that he had radical ideas about education or that it would matter if he had.

Those who wanted the Prince had another motive. They did not want too conservative-looking a Chancellor. The government would be less likely to reform the university high-handedly if it thought that the university was reforming itself. Prince Albert was not identified with any form of ultra-conservatism. His presence as Chancellor would prevent radical change but make them look vaguely liberal in intention, which would be politically desirable.

Prince Albert agreed to be elected Chancellor, on condition that the election was unanimous. This condition was already impossible. The Earl of Powis had been invited to stand for election almost simultaneously. He was an ultra-conservative peer of no distinction whatever, who had the merit that he would try to keep the university as it was and the demerit that he might make the government think the University of Cambridge to be incorrigible in its determination not to be changed, and therefore invite interference from outside.

The Queen's husband could not compete. 'Very unbecoming and indecorous' was how the Queen described the idea of a contest. Prince Albert withdrew from the battle.

He had second thoughts. His advisers considered that to withdraw betrayed nerves to the nation and might harm his image more than a contest. They told Cambridge that he had refused to stand; but that this did not mean that he would not accept if he were elected. This distinction seemed metaphysical. But the Prince's advisers, and his Cambridge committee, were confident that in a contest with Lord Powis he would be elected easily.

Their confidence was misplaced. The invention of the railway shifted the balance of power in the constitution of both the older universities. Every graduate had a vote in the election. Formerly the residents decided because it was too far for others to travel. Now the non-residents counted, and many of them were intellectual troglodytes. But so were some, though fewer, of the residents.

As a candidate in a popular election (though he was not a candidate) Prince Albert gave a chance to that part of the press which disliked him. *Punch* was the *Private Eye* of that day. It did its best to render Prince Albert ludicrous, and portrayed the

members of the university as contemptible flatterers, and their
leaders as clergymen scrambling for bishoprics. It described how
at the rite of installation all the heads of colleges would prostrate
themselves upon the ground –

> Your disregard of scholarship you boldly did evince,
> With the dignity of Chancellor when you adorned a Prince.

These gibes hardly helped Lord Powis. But to the end some voters
thought that the Chancellor of Cambridge must be an Englishman
and a Cambridge man. Dr George Corrie, who was not famous for
an open mind, described Prince Albert as 'an exalted personage,
who has not been educated among us, nor even nurtured in our
Church'.

The election was conducted amid the cries and catcalls of horn-
blowing and peashooting undergraduates. The Prince won by
only 117 votes and wondered whether the size of the minority
should make him refuse. Fortunately for the university he
accepted.

Fortunately, because unlike many previous Chancellors he
actually wanted to make the university better.

In the installation ode, supposedly written by the poet laureate
Wordsworth but actually heaped together by a deputy in Wordsworth's last decline, the Prince was pictured as presiding

> in these collegiate bowers
> Where science, leagued with holier truth,
> Guards the sacred heart of youth.

But science had almost nothing to do with Cambridge truth and
they could hardly learn the holier truth of divinity unless Greek
be regarded as divinity. He found his new university a strange
place.

The Fellows of King's College were the strangest of all. On
their admission they had to swear that they would propose no
changes in their statutes nor accept changes when proposed by
others; and therefore their statutes were an archaic cloak for a
shocking series of abuses – as for example, they claimed that all

their students could proceed to a university degree without passing any of the examinations of the University. It was a right, or claim, which they cheerfully sacrificed at last while Prince Albert was Chancellor. The Master of Clare rid himself of a Fellow of Clare because the Fellow was also a professor in Scotland, and because his subscription to the Church of Scotland as a professor disagreed with his subscription to the Church of England as a Fellow. An appeal to Prince Albert (as Chancellor he was Visitor of Clare College) was referred to assessors in Cambridge who held the Master to be unjustified. The German in Albert must have found all this hard to comprehend.

The Prince very soon found that it was awkward to have to be political as Chancellor and non-political as a Prince. This awkwardness was typical of his entire predicament in British life, and the way in which he handled it was typical of his skill in judging what was possible and what was not. Occasionally he was afterwards inclined to wonder whether he had done right to allow himself to be elected Chancellor. But by remaining behind the scenes, by exerting his influence privately, by seeing that he was well-informed, by an excellent judgement on moderate and wise men to serve him and draft his public speeches, he had no need to worry.

The government wanted to appoint a Commission to inquire into Cambridge. The University did not want a Commission. Prince Albert was expected to agree with the University. At least he could hardly say that he disagreed. Yet privately he was sure that the University needed reforming. He preferred that it should reform itself, but if that was impossible – and he soon saw that it was hardly possible – he was not willing to stand up against a Commission. This placed him in a very delicate situation. He was even insulted in the House of Lords by the Chancellor of Oxford University, the Duke of Wellington, who said that though the University of Oxford intended to effect every desirable improvement, it did not intend to introduce German methods of education.

Introduction

Rude or not, the remark pointed to a special difficulty of the Prince's position. Two ideals of a university were beginning to compete for the allegiance, and the right to preserve or change the structures, of the two medieval English universities. One was the teaching collegiate ideal of Oxford, enshrined only two years later in Newman's *Lectures* at Dublin, where *The Idea of a University* is framed in terms of a Mount Zion which owes its earthly image to memories of all that was best in the University of Oxford; and the ideal which was at the moment called (with suspicion) 'German', where professors and their 'research' made the essential of the university, and the college tutor would become a very subordinate animal. The Prime Minister Lord John Russell wrote to the Prince a letter in which he compared Fellows of Colleges to the occupants of old pocket boroughs of the past, an old abuse which rightful reform could sweep away; and compared them further to old landlords making money out of the poor before the repeal of the corn laws. This was a courteously phrased brutality to a Prince who was Chancellor of a university full of Fellows of Colleges. Yet he himself had studied at a German university and saw its merits. His university expected him, a German, to defend them against the incoming of German ideals.

He persuaded the Prime Minister to refrain from his Commission. He persuaded the University to appoint a committee (syndicate) to reform itself. When nevertheless the government, two years later, appointed the Commission after all, the Queen thought it a cavalier treatment of her husband. Nevertheless, far wiser than the Duke of Wellington at Oxford, he was not willing to advise his University to resist the operations of the Commission, even at the risk that diehards in Cambridge would regard him as a traitor and unworthy of his office. This was courageous and was carried out with skill. Incidentally he greatly pleased the Prime Minister.

When the matter is considered in hindsight, the inexperienced Prince was wiser than the experienced Duke of Wellington. The

7

one fatal policy would be to refuse to give evidence to the Commission, and force government to reform the universities with the aid of opinions unrepresentative of the universities. Resentment in both Oxford and Cambridge was already fostering the doctrine that refusal to cooperate would be the right policy. Many regarded the Commission as unconstitutional. To cooperate would be to recognise it as constitutional. Wellington's attitude encouraged, Prince Albert's attitude discouraged, non-cooperation. There is no doubt now which university had the Chancellor more helpful to its longer-term interests.

At this moment it was particularly unfortunate that the new Vice-Chancellor, in November 1849, was the Master of Jesus College, Dr George Corrie, who was an extreme non-cooperator and strongly disapproved of the Chancellor of his University. Hitherto relations between the Chancellor and four successive Vice-Chancellors had been delightful. The Prince invited them in turn to dinner, a hospitality which no previous Chancellor was believed to have practised. Philpott, the Master of St Catharine's, became his chief resident adviser and informant on Cambridge affairs. All this was now changed. Corrie, though beloved by a small circle of friends, was an absurd, eccentric and obstinate man. He was also extremely shy and timid. He took pains to see that he should not be invited by the Prince to dinner, lest his refusal of the invitation offend. It was believed that his curious refusal before being invited has a part-origin in his extreme shyness and terror at the idea of meeting his Queen. But this was not the only reason. He declared that 'the Royal Commission... has not made the Court popular among us'. He attributed the Royal Commission to 'a mischievous spirit of meddling by some'.

Dr Corrie did not attend the Prince when he presented an address on behalf of the University to the Queen. The occasion was emotional. The Pope created Catholic dioceses in England, and the country was aflame. The University of Cambridge passed an address to the Queen declaring its deep concern that 'the

8

Bishop of Rome has arrogated to himself the right to intermeddle with the government of our country and to ignore the ancient episcopacy of our Church...By this unwarrantable assumption of power on the part of the Bishop of Rome, not only are your Majesty's high prerogative and the lawful authority and jurisdiction of the prelates of our Church invaded and outraged, but the consciences of your Majesty's loyal subjects are grievously offended.' Whatever the Prince thought of this, he had to read it to his wife solemnly, as the sentiment of his university, at a Windsor wrapt in thick fog.

In private, he thought very ill of the drafting of the address. He protested to Henry Philpott about the wording and Philpott agreed that it was a miserable production unworthy of the occasion. It cannot have made the Prince more enthusiastic to find that the drafter of this address was Dr Corrie. Dr Corrie started as a member of the procession from Windsor town to the Castle. But as they approached, he could be seen hurrying away, and absented himself from the ceremony. One theory attributed this extraordinary desertion to a sudden fit of shyness, another to a sudden fit of diarrhoea.

The Queen's reply was dignified and conceded nothing to prejudice. But the Prince never afterwards read to his wife any address by the University of Cambridge. Evidently he did not like to have words which he personally disapproved put into his mouth.

Meanwhile the work of reform went forward with his encouragement from behind the scenes. He wanted wider studies, not only classics and mathematics; and the university founded triposes of moral sciences (philosophy) and of natural sciences. The development of the natural sciences in what was to become one of the leading scientific universities of the world owed most to the mathematical excellence long in the Cambridge tradition, but owed something also to Prince Albert. He wanted a school of theology but could not get it, and only got a voluntary examination in theology. He wanted no undergraduate to be able to take a degree without receiving some instruction in modern history, and the plan never had a chance. Henry Philpott advised him that persons aged eighteen to twenty-one are not capable of studying everything at once, and that because so many of them were going to be country parsons they needed the Greek language more than they needed history. However history also became an optional course. Very few people took these optional courses. But they existed, and could grow.

Prince Albert wanted university education to be cheaper and saw that colleges were expensive ways of education. His experience in Germany did not lead him to think colleges essential. Oxford accepted the plan, that an undergraduate might study at Oxford though not a member of a college. Cambridge did not. The Chancellor of Cambridge nevertheless pushed a clause into the university bill in Parliament making it possible, but without result. He shared in this matter the views of advanced reformers, mainly religious men, who wanted to open the old universities to a wider social class. Cambridge replied that colleges were not expensive, that scholarships or sizarships were available to the poor, and that students not in a college would be sure to be undisciplined. The refusal deeply disappointed Prince Albert. He was never quite satisfied with the way in which his university conducted its onward march of progress.

He wanted more lecture rooms and better museums. He offered to contribute to the expense. He believed in competition as good for the studies of the young, and established an annual prize for legal studies, and chose the subjects for the annual prize for an English poem (for example, 'on the late Queen Adelaide').

He liked to have his special correspondents in Cambridge. Naturally the Vice-Chancellor wrote to him on official business. But the office of Vice-Chancellor was held by the heads of colleges in turn and changed every year or every two years; and therefore the relation between Chancellor and Vice-Chancellor changed with each occupant of the latter office. When Henry Philpott, Master of St Catharine Hall, was Vice-Chancellor, the alliance was very close because Philpott was in any case one of his two favourite Cambridge correspondents. When George Corrie, the Master of Jesus College, was Vice-Chancellor, communications between Chancellor and Vice-Chancellor were as distant and formal as possible. Philpott was a sensible man, and served Prince Albert and the University with fair reporting and wise advice.

On 19 January 1861 Philpott was nominated to be the new Bishop of Worcester. That pleased the Queen and the Prince, but meant that the Prince lost his chief Cambridge adviser. Prince Albert told Philpott that he wanted to appoint, from among the Fellows of Cambridge Colleges, a chaplain who should take on the duty of being his correspondent in the university and sending him the material which it was important for him to know. Philpott selected the young Fellow of Trinity College, Joseph Barber Lightfoot, later to become one of the greatest of Victorian historians and perhaps its greatest divine. The choice was excellent. And for the remaining months until the Prince's death, Lightfoot was his chaplain with the duty of sending him information about the activities of the University. He discharged these duties faithfully. The Prince continued to receive fair-minded information.

The Chancellor knew prudent moderate men when he saw them. His other Cambridge correspondent was quainter, but his selection also says something about the mind of the Prince. He was Adam Sedgwick, the professor of geology, and one of the Senior Fellows of Trinity College.

The Prince made him 'Chancellor's Secretary', as a formal office. The post was even announced in the newspapers. The Prince perhaps imagined beforehand that Sedgwick would do for him what Philpott did, send sensible reports on routine affairs. But Sedgwick was not like that. He was an eccentric, one of the Cambridge characters of the nineteenth century. Nothing about his letters could ever be routine. They were colourful, extraordinary, gossipy, conversational. Nothing in them was dull. He discoursed entertainingly or tragically of his gout, or his influenza, or his injuries; of the bizarre conduct of the Vice-Chancellor, or the absurd opinions of narrow conservatives; and seriously but still amusingly of science, and his need for a museum, and fossils and the skeleton of a prehistoric monster.

He was not precisely an adviser because he seldom advised. Compared with the routine of Philpott who was so sensible that he was nearly dull, Sedgwick rambled enchantingly into byways, and so could hardly influence the policy of a Prince. Nevertheless he was important to the Prince, who was determined to encourage the natural sciences in Cambridge and realised that geology was the fertile science of that generation. When Prince Albert paid a formal visit to the University in 1853 he (or the University) over-loaded his programme monstrously, so that he rushed hither and thither with hardly time to 'inspect' the colleges or university institutions through which he passed. But he took the time to attend a whole lecture on geology by Adam Sedgwick.

When Prince Albert was influencing the composition of the Royal Commission inquiring into the University and wanted to pack that Commission with moderate reforming scientists, he made a point of seeing that Sedgwick was invited to serve, and then another point of seeing that Sedgwick, who had about his rugged frame a touch of the coy prima donna, should not refuse the invitation. When the Commission was over, he probably had a hand in seeing that the Crown rewarded Sedgwick with the offer of the deanery of Peterborough; an offer which, mercifully for both Cambridge and Peterborough, Sedgwick refused.

The longer he was Chancellor the more detailed material his correspondents sent him, realising that it was not waste paper but that he was concerned and would try to make time to read it and sometimes to comment. In the later years they sent him not merely formal papers arising out of the reform of studies or of the constitution, but lists of lectures and even sets of examination papers and the number and quality of candidates entered for the newer triposes which he had helped to found.

He wanted professors to be more important in the university, and he wanted better professors. This was very difficult to achieve because many of the Cambridge chairs were so ill-endowed that a man could not hold them unless he had other work or had a lot of money of his own. The Prince wanted to force the colleges to contribute from their historic endowments to the poor university and thereby help it to endow the professorships better. But meanwhile his anxieties over the filling of certain chairs were not small. And apart from the difficulty over money, he suspected with reason that professors were sometimes chosen for reasons which were not purely academic; and that a grave offender in this matter was the Prime Minister.

His predicament is shown by the troubles over the chair of modern history. This chair was very important to the Prince; it represented one of those wider studies which he wanted to encourage. When he became Chancellor its holder was Professor Smyth, who had held the chair for forty years and was now so ancient that he did not lecture at all; and indeed there was hardly any reason why the professor should lecture since no undergraduates would come to his lectures, as they could not, before Prince Albert's reforms, count history even among optional courses.

Professor Smyth, once tutor to Sheridan, and venerable relic of a Napoleonic age, died at last in 1849. Even before he died, the Prince consulted Thomas Babington Macaulay about his successor. The Chancellor caused three leading possibilities for the professorship to draft a statement on their expected courses and hopes if they were appointed. The Prince therefore was bitterly disappointed when Lord John Russell preferred to use the post for a political job, finding a convenient home for Sir James Stephen so that he might still be able to give advice to the Colonial Office. Sir James Stephen had written *Essays in Ecclesiastical Biography* but the Prime Minister was perfectly frank that this had not been the ultimate motive for his selection. The Prince even tried to overtrump the Queen's Prime Minister by acting for once high-handedly and directly offering the chair (which he had no right to do) to Macaulay himself – correctly judging that if Macaulay accepted not even Lord John Russell had the impertinence to go on pressing Stephen. But Macaulay was respectful and resolute in declining. So Stephen had the chair, and the Prince was quite rude to the Prime Minister.

The Prince could not help being wryly, perhaps even naughtily, amused at the Prime Minister's discomfiture when the new professor was immediately accused of gnostic heresies in a public pamphlet and was forced to exculpate himself. 'Who would have thought' smilingly asked Dr George Corrie, who disapproved of Lord John Russell and jested that *in healthier times* he would have paid for his politics with his head, 'that we should have seen a live gnostic walking about the streets of Cambridge...In healthier times he would have been burnt.'

Only one hour a week could be allotted to modern history, and neither the system nor the appointment pleased Prince Albert.

When Professor Stephen died in 1860 the choice was equally difficult. Lord Palmerston consulted Macaulay, now Lord Macaulay. When two men in succession refused, the despairing Lord Palmerston asked Prince Albert to consult opinion in Cambridge. This method only produced a third refusal. The post certainly did not seem to be keenly wanted. It was then that the Prince himself suggested to the Prime Minister the name of Charles Kingsley the historical novelist; and Palmerston, consulting, was told that Kingsley was a 'great unknown' but that he was probably very fit for the work of the professor. Kingsley was also a keen amateur scientist and understood the history of the relations of science and religion and this undoubtedly attracted the Prince, who did not live long enough to see that the novelist and popular lecturer in him triumphed over the historian in him and that the selection was not a success.

14

Introduction

In 1853, in person in the Senate House, the Prince gave an honorary degree to his relative, the heir to the throne of Belgium. It was noticed that his Latin used a different formula from the usual. Instead of the Chancellor's normal *auctoritate mihi commissa* ('by the authority entrusted to me') he said *auctoritate qua fungimur* ('by the authority which we possess'). Evidently his ideas of the Chancellorship did not expect authority to come from below.

Cambridge never found him familiar. Always he was reserved, royal, a man of dignity. But they found him modest, and with no inflated idea of his powers or his pretensions. He had not the light and easy touch which wins the applause of a crowd, but they came to admire the steady and prudent benevolence of the man; never sentimental, never up in the clouds, always practical in his quest for the better, and, despite the reserve and the dignity, content to do good by stealth and without desire to take public credit for what he achieved.

He never quite got over the feeling that they were behind the times. And usually he was right. Just occasionally he mistook old custom for the hidebound. After the reform, he was surprised to discover that the University intended to keep its legislation in the Latin language. He thought this habit affected and absurd and did not hide his opinion. But the University preferred to keep its custom. Adam Sedgwick knew how to handle this feeling. On occasions like this he would freely lament that the University crept on at the pace of a paralytic, but at least it crept.

When the Prince died the Regius Professor of Divinity, Dr Jeremie, preached a more emotional, even a more tearful, sermon than would have been customary a few decades later. But the quiet respect for a benefactor of the first rank, who had no need to be a benefactor at all, comes through the language of the orator.

He was not a mere sentimental and speculative, but a real and practical reformer...We perceive...how mildness was allied with energy, how zeal was

15

tempered with prudence, how noiseless quietness was united with unceasing activity, and the most enlightened discrimination with the warmest benevolence and patriotism...The Prince Consort never sought the fugitive applause of the multitude. His modesty, his dignified reserve forbad any approach to familiarity...Yet see the homage which is paid to right principles and right motives... For many years the Prince Consort had presided over it [this University] with that intelligence and consummate prudence, which marked and adorned his character. We imagine that we still see among us that form of grace – that countenance of calm and placid dignity, on which all that breathes of high thoughts and gentle deeds was impressed.

THE LEGACY OF
PRINCE ALBERT

H.R.H. THE DUKE OF GLOUCESTER

THERE are several reasons why I should be interested in the story of Prince Albert; the most relevant is that he was my great-great-grandfather and the most irrelevant is the coincidence that we share a birthdate. But in spite of the 120 years that separate us, it is difficult not to see him as a person with a very modern outlook, a man who would be able to understand present-day problems much better than would his contemporaries. So to me, he becomes much easier to appreciate as a personality than other historical characters from bygone eras. He is also easy to research because of the very many documents – both official and private correspondence – which are available for historians to consult, and which clarify any confusion which his full life occasions.

He was born on 26 August 1819, Prince Albert of Saxe-Coburg and Gotha, the younger son of Duke Ernest. He was heir to no fortune, and his home could boast little to distinguish it from the forty or so other principalities that constituted Germany at that time. Yet Roger Fulford, a biographer of Prince Albert, described him as being by 1840 'the most eligible bachelor in Europe'. How could such an assertion be made when there were crowds of princes with greater wealth and territorial possessions?

First of all let us consider how successful the Coburg family dynastic marriage policy was. Albert's father, Duke Ernest, was the eldest of a large family: one of his sisters married first, a Prince Leiningen, and in her widowhood, the Duke of Kent, a younger brother of the British King George IV – not a very auspicious match it would seem at the time. Her brother Léopold was more successful because he married the King's only daughter Charlotte, heir to the British throne; but tragically she died in childbirth eighteen months later, leaving Prince Léopold with nothing to do but contemplate what might have been, and his annuity of £50,000 for life. Fortunately for him, the Catholic part of the Low Countries wanted a constitutional monarch, and he accepted their offer to become King of the Belgians.

Léopold's loss was his sister's gain, for her daughter, Victoria, was the heir after her Uncle William; and the Coburgs now had a Belgian and a British throne to add to that of Portugal in their collection.

Albert's father had married a girl much younger than himself, and it became apparent that his motives had been mainly to acquire her principality of Gotha rather than to create a flourishing family home. Albert was only five when his mother left her faithless husband, and he never saw her again, for she died a few years later of cancer. It was no doubt this experience of a child's sense of loss that made him for ever conscious of the need for family unity and the dangers of self-indulgence and immorality. Although he often referred to his childhood as 'paradise', he was really referring to the beauty of Coburg, and the opportunities he had to grow up both in the countryside and in a lively town, rather than to the kind of happy home life which he was later able to provide for his own children.

There was a certain doctor in Coburg, who had been a long-standing family friend, who recognised Albert's superior intelligence at an early age and sought to shield him from the dangerous influence of his father by subjecting the boy to more wholesome influences. This same doctor, later to become Baron Stockmar, also exerted an influence on the upbringing of Princess Victoria in England and frequently visited King Léopold, now the epitome of a constitutional monarch.

It would seem, given this combination, that Victoria and Albert were destined to be married, and Stockmar ensured that in every way his choice for Victoria should be a suitable one: a Coburg educated to be analytical, efficient, logical, well versed in music and the arts. The fact that Albert was handsome and athletic made him more attractive than ever. It was also most convenient that he was a Protestant, and as a younger son would not be encumbered with German responsibilities as the Hanoverian kings had been until they became independent again with Victoria's accession. The good doctor had thought of everything.

When Victoria and Albert came to meet, they made a mutually favourable impression although they were both only seventeen. The next year Victoria became Queen; and she enjoyed the freedom this gave her so much that she nearly forgot all about Albert. King Léopold and Stockmar realised that the only remedy was to bring them together again. So Prince Albert returned to London in October 1839, and five days later Queen Victoria 'with becoming modesty and an emphasis on the drawbacks of the offer she was making, which did her the greatest credit, asked for Prince Albert's hand. He accepted.'

The reaction of the British public was the opposite to that of Victoria and Albert, who were delighted with each other. Albert did not seem nearly grand enough for a public which was still enjoying the thought of a young girl on the throne after many years of the old brothers George and William. One critic gibed:

> He comes the bridegroom of Victoria's choice,
> The nominee of Lehzen's vulgar voice,
> He comes to take, 'for better or for worse',
> England's fat Queen and England's fatter purse.

The purse was not to be as fat as Albert might have hoped, for it would be expected that The Queen's Consort should have an annuity of £50,000 a year, as Prince Léopold still did, and as had Prince George, the husband of Queen Anne, in 1690. However, Parliament was uncooperative, and voted only £30,000 a year.

In this respect Albert was unlucky to be a Coburg, because there was resentment in Protestant England at Léopold taking his £50,000 and then becoming king of a Roman Catholic country.

Naturally, such an insulting beginning was highly mortifying to the Prince, considering that, only twenty at the time, he was leaving home and country not just to get married but to take up a career the unique nature of which no one, least of all himself, could have envisaged.

The only precedent for a husband of a British Queen-Regnant had been Prince George of Denmark, a man remarkable only for his general affability and his contentment at having no apparent function other than that of making his loving wife, Queen Anne, frequently pregnant, although tragically they never produced a healthy heir.

It would seem that everyone had assumed, as Queen Victoria herself assumed, that Albert would be her spouse, lover and companion, but in no way her co-regnant; and that their marriage would be like that of most other couples but with the rôles reversed: 'I am only the husband and not the master in the house', Albert wrote to Stockmar.

In fact it was fortunate for both of them that they were so young, inexperienced and lacking in confidence; for Albert had to fight for his right to be master in his house. He wisely began by gaining the love and trust of his wife in their life together, and slowly, step by step, involving himself in her work as Sovereign. Initially he just held the blotting paper while she signed papers, but all the time he was learning, and his efficient and analytical mind was working out how he could best help her. He knew that to help the woman he loved he must make himself indispensable as her adviser on many different matters; he knew he had the ability and the energy; and he saw no good reason why he should allow his ignorance to debar him from any field, when a little research and application could well bring him up to date on any matter at issue.

The first problem he had to solve was in many ways the most

complex, for he felt that his wife was being most badly advised on how a constitutional monarch should relate to her Government. It is difficult to imagine many men in their early twenties – newly arrived in a strange country – asking both the Prime Minister and the Monarch to examine this fundamental problem in a new light; but with great courage and perseverance he did so, and over the years all concerned came to thank him for it.

Political innovation absorbed but part of his energies, which were considerable. He completely restructured the running of Buckingham Palace and Windsor Castle – long overdue reforms that caused a lot of ill will from those who benefited from past inefficiency.

The frustrations of living in houses administered by bureaucratic government departments led to Victoria and Albert wanting a home of their own. They chose a place as far south as possible but yet in reach of London, and Albert designed a house for them as similar as possible to the Italian villas he had admired on the Mediterranean. Inevitably the project became an ambitious one, but the Prince thrived on challenges of this kind, and his creation at Osborne is known for its subtlety of design, distinctive silhouette and skilful landscaping rather than for any delicacy of detail.

His second building project was at Balmoral, in the Highlands of Scotland. This was on a smaller scale, and in a romantic Scottish style of beautifully cut granite. Anyone who has stayed there will confirm that it is built for comfort and convenience rather than grandeur, and its great charm lies in the informality of its arrangement.

The Prince's first public appointment outside the Royal Household was as Chairman of a Royal Commission to decide how the new Houses of Parliament were to be decorated. The consequence of this appointment does not seem either startling or exciting today, but its chief success can be measured by the fact that the public exhibition that was held to show the submissions by various artists was visited by no less than 500,000 people – an unusual interest in government as a patron of the arts.

Prince Albert himself painted, as did Queen Victoria. Although he was modest enough to regard the process as being of more value than the end-product, he was also very knowledgeable about art history, and one of his most prized projects was reorganising the royal collection of drawings concentrating on Raphael's works, of which he made an historical study. He also bought paintings either from the early Renaissance or the late Gothic period, or contemporary works that appealed to him. His patronage of the arts won him no greater esteem than the collections of his predecessors, but his attitude to the desire for collecting was different. He did not claim to be an originator in artistic terms, but saw his value not as a private collector but as a populariser, bringing to the public's attention the part that artists in general can play in a person's visual comprehension of the world. He organised a large exhibition on the history of art which he chose to display in Manchester, which at that time was a centre both for industry and for civil unrest and seemed therefore to him to be in most need of this sudden cultural infusion.

It is this that makes him appear such a contemporary rather than an historical character: he saw – maybe naively – that his rôle as the Queen's husband was not to seek for self-aggrandisement but to strive quietly to achieve those things which his high principles led him to believe were worthwhile for the good of his wife's people. He believed that an appreciation of the visual arts and an understanding of the principles of design were of benefit to everyone and a necessity in an age of ever-greater material productivity. This belief led eventually to the creation of a series of Design and Art Schools and the creation of a new kind of popular museum – as opposed to the old kind typified by the British Museum, which at that time was very much an academics' club which the public was discouraged from visiting and the masses actually debarred unless suitably dressed.

To read of Prince Albert's life is rather like hearing a well-constructed but abrasive Sunday sermon. However much one questions his judgement, one would never call him a hypocrite. For instance he was always a very staunch believer in the necessity for a free press, although he was, throughout his life, attacked viciously in the British press and accused of the most amazing things, but most consistently of being an interfering foreigner, who could not possibly have British interests at heart.

Another reason why the Prince appears such a contemporary figure lies in his understanding of the aims of science. His own high principles – however naive – led him to believe in 'truth' as an ideal, and he saw the study of all science, whether physics, chemistry, biology, medicine or statistics, as being entirely in the cause of progress, and that any unfortunate side effects were the result of wrong application rather than an over-reliance on novelty. It is for this reason that he got on so much better with the new Victorian technologists, who were using the new science to advance industry to make Great Britain the leading industrial nation. To them, all problems would in time be solved by new methods and greater understanding. To them, as for Albert, technology was the solution to mankind's problems rather than just a technique of making wealth to maintain the power and prestige of individuals.

Education was inevitably another interest – he was elected Chancellor of Cambridge University as a result of the favourable impression he made there when he accompanied Queen Victoria on a visit. Both Oxford and Cambridge were at that time very old-fashioned and conservative. Theology, classics and mathematics were still the main subjects taught. It was obvious that it was time for reform, but the traditionalists were well entrenched. Prince Albert was able to persuade them that it was better to introduce change from within rather than wait for outside pressures to build up. It is difficult to evaluate how much his influence affected the issue but, during his Chancellorship, Cambridge widened its horizons to provide an education much more like that with which Prince Albert was familiar in Germany. Oxford followed suit, but I still feel that Cambridge is even today more receptive to new educational ideas than Oxford.

Prince Albert was an accomplished musician – it becomes almost embarrassing to list his versatility. He found playing the organ a great relaxation from the stress that inevitably filled his day. Music appealed strongly to his emotions, affecting that sentimental nature which he so often referred to. Under his care, the tradition of Court concerts expanded greatly, and instead of being cautiously conservative represented the most up-to-date music and the greatest musicians of his day. Prince Albert introduced Bach to England, where he had been almost unknown, and of course Mendelssohn was a frequent and favourite visitor.

I have already mentioned that Prince Albert was athletic – it had been his abilities on the dance floor that had enchanted Queen Victoria when they first met. Indeed one of the most significant alterations made to Buckingham Palace was the addition of a ballroom of suitable dimensions for waltzing, a pleasure that had been curtailed in the older narrow halls and galleries.

He was good at fencing, at swimming and skating; and you will not be surprised to hear that he rode well and was a most accurate shot. Shooting birds with a shotgun did not enthrall him as much as it did most of his descendants, but stalking deer appealed to him immensely, and explains his choice of Balmoral for a summer home.

What he really enjoyed most was a full family life – he loved Victoria because she was such a warm-hearted, affectionate person. There is no doubt that he found her intelligent but ill-informed and badly educated – it clearly gave them both great pleasure that he was able to teach her so much and bring out her latent talents by careful application of his instructive ability. Initially, of course, there were tensions, misunderstandings, rows and sulks, as with many a young married couple; but the intensity of their relationship brought them ever closer together, and the joy they shared with their children was something that made this a very closeknit family, come what may. However, Albert's high principles meant that duty always came before pleasure: indeed it was said of him that he 'could not resist duty' and he was forever working on several improving projects at once.

One of the advantages of having so many accomplishments was that he was sometimes able to identify several problems that could be solved by the same solution. His most successful attempt at this was the Great Exhibition. It came about because Prince Albert wanted to do two quite different things. Having travelled about his new country and seen for himself the variations between North and South and East and West, he was struck by the provincial nature of the places he visited, and saw how it prevented many British people from appreciating how successful the country was collectively. Similarly he wanted to sell the idea of a liberal constitutional monarchy to many foreigners, and he saw the idea of the Great Exhibition as being both an advertisement for the British way of life and a demonstration of its richness of ability and invention.

In the event he was blessed by having the finest nineteenth-century structure suddenly thrown up, virtually overnight, in Hyde Park. The architecture of the Crystal Palace itself dazzled every visitor by its immensity and its simplicity. The timing was also fortunate, for the new railway lines made London accessible by 1851 to literally millions of British people, who came, mostly travelling long distances, and for the first time in their lives.

The effect on British morale was electric, and the lesson to the many foreign visitors, who were attracted by its international prestige, was also salutary – not, of course, that the exhibition had the hoped-for effect of bringing peace to the world.

Prince Albert was not the sole originator of the Great Exhibition, but as Chairman he deserved the credit he got for its success both popular and financial. The profits went to pay for the future Victoria and Albert Museum.

It is perhaps assumed by many people that to say that someone is a monarchist is to imply that he must be reactionary and conservative. Albert was a monarchist – and why not? After all, Switzerland was the only European country without a monarchy at that time, and it was racked with regional dissension. But he was an 'improving monarchist': he did not believe that a monarch should merely represent the *status quo*, but rather that he or she should be constantly working for the greater good of the country in particular, and for world peace in general. There was no time in his book for a monarch who took the privileges of that position for granted, or sought for self-glorification by taking credit for another man's achievements or for seeking scapegoats for his own failings. Similarly he had no time for self-indulgence, believing strongly that the highest in the land should set a good example and live by the highest standards of morality. He was made well aware of the consequences of following the slippery path of dalliance by the examples of his father and brother and some of his wife's 'wicked' uncles.

Inevitably, when a man attempts so many different things he must expect his share of failures; and it is sad to relate that his most spectacular failure was the one which perhaps lay nearest to his heart, apart from his immediate family. It grew from the great love he had for his own country. To him Germany was a great country, populated by hard-working, diligent and intelligent people – held back by the multiplicity of its small states, whose petty jealousies consumed the energy that could have produced the most civilised, the most cultured, the most creative people in Europe. His dream was for a Germany united, like the United States of America, with all the different monarchies existing, but serving under an Emperor. He saw that that Emperor would have to be either Prussian or Austrian, and he favoured Prussia because of Austria's non-German responsibilities. But it was a vital element of his plan that it should be a Prussia influenced by the rest of Germany rather than Germany Prussianised. It was of course a dream; but he believed that just possibly he was himself in the unique position to be able to bring this about, and particularly so if he could but induce his new country to help him, for he felt that Britain and a united Germany were more naturally allied and shared more interests than France or Russia or any of the other nation states.

It was because he held this dream so dear that he was prepared to see his eldest daughter, whom he loved perhaps more dearly than all his children, leave home at the age of seventeen to go to live in Berlin as the wife of the heir to the Prussian throne, Crown Prince Friedrich. Princess Victoria, or Vicky as she was called, was his 'secret weapon' to bring about this dream, for she was not only very pretty with a lively attractive personality, she was also extremely intelligent and under his parental guidance educated to be almost a carbon copy of himself. For her part, she was happy to set out on this venture, for she worshipped her father and all he stood for. Like him, she saw the necessity to sacrifice one's pleasure for an ideal and to see one's duty as improving the lot of the people before anything else.

Within four years of her marriage to Prince Friedrich, who regarded Prince Albert with the same veneration as his wife, Prince Albert died. Vicky found that instead of being part of a team, she was suddenly the captain and only full-time member. Shortly after this, her father-in-law handed Prussia over to Bismarck. Germany was to become unified, not in the way Albert intended, through diplomacy, but by 'blood and iron'.

Vicky and her husband bided their time, and endured Bismarck's malevolence with the knowledge that one day her Fritz would be Kaiser, and things could then change. But Fritz's father lived to be ninety, and fate was to strike Fritz down with cancer, so his reign lasted but a hundred days. Vicky had lost the loyalty of her son to Bismarck, and thus she was totally deprived of the opportunity to put forward the plans of her father, her husband and herself for a modern liberal Germany allied closely to Great

Britain. To wonder what would have happened if the Kaiser Friedrich III had lived his allotted span is to be convinced that the First World War might never have happened, and consequently the Second World War avoided, which has resulted in a Germany divided even more severely than it was in Prince Albert's day.

But to return to Prince Albert's successes – what is the one thing which I have to thank him for most? I believe it is for identifying the ideal relationship between a monarch and his country, and for trying so very hard to show how it is possible to live up to that ideal; how it is possible to lead a harmonious family life in spite of the intrusions and frequently the inventions of the press and other disruptive influences; how it is possible to get satisfaction from doing something as well as one can, whether other people appreciate it or not; and a belief that ultimately duty comes first.

It was a lesson well learnt by his descendants, and I feel it most appropriate that I should be referring to it here in Coburg: the very place where he grew up and experienced some of the joys and the adversities that formed a character that was such an influence for good.

I sincerely hope that you will enjoy hearing about and discussing him during this seminar, and I hope he will be recognised as a pioneer of Anglo-German understanding, and therefore of value to those who wish for a strong and united Europe.

THE PRINCE CONSORT
AND QUEEN VICTORIA'S
PRIME MINISTERS

ROBERT BLAKE

BETWEEN his arrival in England in 1840 and his death in 1861 the Prince Consort had dealings with six Prime Ministers. If I may remind you of names and dates, they were: Lord Melbourne, till 1841; Sir Robert Peel, 1841–6; Lord John Russell, 1846–52; Lord Derby, 1852 and again in 1858–9; Lord Aberdeen, 1852–5; Lord Palmerston, 1855–8, and again from 1859 for the brief remainder of the Prince's life. He also knew and had views about the two most famous Prime Ministers of the Queen's later years, Disraeli and Gladstone, though neither reached what Disraeli called 'the top of the greasy pole' in the Prince's lifetime.

The historical significance of the Prince's relations with the Queen's Prime Ministers is the same as whatever historical significance can be accorded to the rôle of the Crown in politics. Although for a brief period after their marriage the Prince was not admitted to the Queen's innermost counsels, from 1841 onward his influence became paramount. Four years later Greville, the famous diarist, could write with truth 'He is the King to all intents and purposes.' The royal marriage was arranged partly for this very purpose – to provide the Queen with a wise adviser. The matchmaker, Léopold of Saxe-Coburg and Gotha and King of the Belgians, was their mutual uncle. He might well have been a Prince Consort himself if his first ·wife, Princess Charlotte, George IV's only daughter, had not died in childbirth. He had given thought to the problems facing the husband of a Queen, and his elevation by popular vote to the Belgian throne in 1831 had caused him to ponder also the problems of 'constitutional monarchy'.

His nephew Albert seemed well suited to the part. As early as 1836 Léopold's Private Secretary, Baron Stockmar, wrote that his youth was balanced by an intelligence which would enable him to give Princess Victoria 'the political support she will one day so badly need', and he added 'in the whole Almanach de Gotha there is not a single Prince of riper years to whom we could entrust the dear child without incurring the gravest risk' – an unflattering but probably not unjust assessment of the Princess's potential suitors. Prince Albert studied hard and worked at his books. His experience of politics was not based merely on obser- vation of Coburg where his father ruled through a rigidly con- servative bureaucracy. The lessons that were printed on his mind came from his uncle's court in Brussels. The anti-Orange revo- lution in the Southern Netherlands had resulted in a monarchy based largely on the English model. The King appointed ministers, but they were responsible to a freely elected legislature. Freedom of the press, of assembly, and of speech, and an independent judiciary were guaranteed.

There was, however, one important difference between the practical operation of the English and Belgian monarchies in the 1830s. In England the Monarch did not pretend to be impartial or to hold the ring between the contending political factions. On the contrary he was a partisan and used his powers to help his party; this partisanship was enhanced by a tradition since the reign of George I that the heir to the throne espoused the opposite party to that favoured by its occupant. George IV from 1812 to his death had been a Tory. His brother William IV was a Whig. He soon became alarmed at Whig reformism and became a Tory, though, after an unsuccessful attempt to oust Lord Melbourne, he had to put up with a Whig government. The Duchess of Kent and her daughter were naturally Whigs. The Duchess particularly disliked the King who had no use for her beloved brother, Léopold, partly because he drank water rather than wine at dinner.

The Coburg attitude to parties, as exemplified by Léopold, was different. The King of the Belgians did not think it right to identify himself with any one party, and his nephew took the same line. The fact that they were both of them foreigners in their respective countries contributed to this attitude. As early as April 1840, only two months after his marriage, Prince Albert put his views on paper:

I do not think it necessary to belong to any party. Composed as party is here of two extremes both must be wrong...The Whigs seek to change *before change is required*. The love of change is their great failing. The Tories on the other hand *resist change* long after the feeling and temper of the times has loudly demanded it...My endeavour will be to form my opinions quite apart from politics and party, and I believe such an attempt may succeed.

His assessment of English parties may seem somewhat naive. Premature change was not likely to come from the Whigs headed by Melbourne, whose favourite remark when one of his colleagues suggested altering anything was: 'Why not let it alone?' On the other side of politics Peel at the head of the Conservatives was to carry out major and timely reforms. Nevertheless the Prince did bring a different attitude to the Crown, whether or not he correctly judged English parties. It is the theme of this lecture that, assisted by events, he succeeded largely but perhaps not entirely in converting the English monarchy from the Hanoverian tradition to what can be called the Coburg model, if one uses Coburg in reference to the Belgian branch of the family, and that his relations with successive Prime Ministers must be seen in that light.

At an early stage he had reason to view with alarm the effects of the partisanship of the court. In November 1839 the Queen told him that she must choose his Household officials and that, in consultation with Melbourne, she had selected as his Private

Secretary, a Whig, George Anson, who performed the same office for Melbourne. The most that the Prince could manage was to get Anson for himself alone, and in the event the arrangement worked well; Anson behaved in an entirely non-partisan way and soon won the Prince's confidence. The second effect of the Queen's Whiggery was more serious. The affair of Lady Flora Hastings and the crisis over the Ladies of the Bedchamber earlier in 1839 convinced the Tories of the hostility of the Court, and in January 1840 with Radical aid they got their own back in the House of Commons by reducing the Prince's annuity from £50,000 to £30,000, and by defeating a Bill to give him precedency next to the Queen. Her pen spluttered with rage as she wrote in her journal 'Vile confounded infernal Tories...Peel...nasty wretch ...Monsters! You Tories shall be punished. Revenge! Revenge!' And she described a leading Tory on the Episcopal Bench as 'that fiend the Bishop of Exeter'.

The Prince, though embarrassed by the episode, bore no malice towards the Tories; for he saw that the Queen had brought the trouble on herself. The question was what he could do. His uncle had told him that he 'ought in business as in everything to be necessary to the Queen, he should be to her a walking dictionary for reference on every point which her own knowledge or education have not enabled her to answer'. Even in favourable circum-stances this was expecting a lot from a young man just married and scarcely over twenty-one. Circumstances were not favourable. One cannot be a walking dictionary of reference for someone who does not wish to refer. The Queen continued to see Melbourne alone or with her former Governess, Baroness Lehzen, and to keep the Prince away from the high affairs of state. Whatever her motive – which was probably a desire not to have to explain everything and answer the Prince's questions – the result was temporarily for the good. The Prince was young; he was very much a foreigner with a strong German accent and un-English manners. To have pushed him to the fore at this early stage might have caused resentments which would have precluded him from playing his valuable later rôle.

Understandably, he did not see this himself. He had no intention of being a mere cipher like Queen Anne's husband Prince George of Denmark in whom, drunk or sober, Charles II said he could find nothing. Prince Albert, it need hardly be said, was always sober. He was also extremely intelligent and imbued with a strong sense of duty. He cannot have been happy at the relations between the Queen and the Prime Minister to whom she had been so deeply devoted ever since her accession. William Lamb, Viscount Melbourne, was still extremely handsome at the age of fifty-eight when the Queen succeeded to the throne in 1837. He was charming, urbane, scholarly, and witty. His private life had been unhappy. His wife had fallen in love with Byron, gone mad and died. His only son and heir, who was mentally handicapped, had predeceased him. These experiences had made him something of a world-weary cynic. People wondered whether he was the right adviser for a youthful Queen. Moralists also had misgivings. In the previous reign he had twice been cited in the divorce courts and, though he was acquitted in each case, his brother after the second wrote to their sister: 'William has got off yet again. No man's luck can go further.'

Melbourne also acted as the Queen's Private Secretary. This key position had been held under William IV by Sir William Taylor. It was part of the reaction against the old régime that it should be abolished and merged with the office of the Prime Minister. Clearly Melbourne had no time to deal with the routine of the post. This fell to Baroness Lehzen, whose possessiveness and jealousy were a major problem for the Prince. It would be wrong, however, to suppose that Melbourne encouraged the Queen to keep her husband away from royal business. On the contrary he urged her to bring him in, and he seriously rebuked Lehzen for standing between husband and wife. The Queen's first pregnancy obliged her to depend more upon the Prince. He made notes on Cabinet business during her confinement, and after the birth of the Princess Royal in November 1840 she gave him, with Melbourne's full agreement, the keys of the confidential boxes.

By the spring of 1841 Melbourne's government began to totter. The Queen was now expecting her second child and the Prince's advice became crucial. At the end of April he sent for Melbourne after the latter had seen the Queen, and urged him to tell her that she must appoint Peel if he (Melbourne) resigned; he added – even more significantly – that from then onwards 'I must be alone her adviser.' Early in May he took another important step. Through Anson he negotiated a compromise with Peel about the position of the Ladies of the Bedchamber and other political Household appointments, in the event of Peel taking office. Melbourne, defeated by one vote on 4 June, half-heartedly advised the Queen to dissolve. This seems to have been the first occasion when the Prince was also present at their meeting. She could – perhaps should – have refused. Defeat in those days was widely regarded as a defeat for the Crown as well as the Prime Minister. Melbourne did not expect to win, though his colleagues were more sanguine. Despite the Prince's doubts, the Queen agreed, probably because there seemed at least a chance of postponing the evil hour of parting with Melbourne. But the election gave a conclusive victory to Peel. In retrospect she thought she had made a mistake. Modern constitutional historians have regarded her view as anachronistic, but by the conventions of the period she was correct in thinking that she had chosen wrongly. Parliament had another three years to run. Hitherto when the Crown had intervened to dissolve, it had always, except in 1835 where the circumstances were not quite the same, secured a win for the sitting government.

Peel's succession went smoothly. The Queen soon got over her misgivings, and the Prince at once found a congenial spirit. Both were serious, intellectual and able. Peel, though a Tory, held 'liberal' views, in the Prince's sense of the words, on fiscal reform, free trade and other matters. He was far from sharing the pre-

judices of the more traditionalist section of his Tory supporters –
in fact so far that in the end the divergence was politically fatal.
There was another favourable factor for Peel. Melbourne represented the quintessence of a highly self-assured Whig aristocracy
many of whose members were wealthier and considered themselves grander than the minor German royal families of which the
Coburgs seemed typical. The Prince had arrived in 1840 on a
political scene dominated by a well-established Prime Minister at
the head of an oligarchy still conscious that its ancestors had
placed the House of Hanover on the throne. Although Peel was
as rich as any of them and had had the same upper-class education,
he was the son of a self-made millionaire and he was socially ill
at ease. When he became Prime Minister the Prince was the well-
established figure whereas Peel was the new man who owed
much to the Prince's support. It is however equally true to say
that the Prince learned a great deal from Peel.

I have dwelt at some length on the events of 1841, for they
constitute the turning-point in the Prince's career. With the
departure of Melbourne he became in practice if not in name the
Queen's Secretary as well as her husband, but he was a Secretary
in a very different position from any before or since. Henceforth
he was always present when she saw any of her Ministers. He was
her principal political adviser and as time went on his domination
became ever greater.

On one matter, however, he could not prevail. The Queen,
despite his advice and that of Stockmar, insisted on continuing
to correspond with Melbourne. Obviously there was a danger
here, but to argue that it was 'unconstitutional' was excessive.
The Prince expressed repeated alarm, but if he had seen the
letters he would have been reassured. Melbourne made no serious
attempt to undermine Peel, and it is hard not to sympathise with
his anger when the Prince and Stockmar, via Anson, lectured
him on the undesirability of a visit to Windsor just after he had
attacked the Government in the House of Lords. Anson wrote:

'He rushed up and across the room in a violent frenzy "God eternally Damn it etc. etc. Flesh and blood could not bear that."' But as time went on the Queen wrote less and less, and Melbourne, becoming ever more eccentric, fades from history – one of the oddest and somehow also one of the most lovable of Prime Ministers.

The Prince's view of parties had largely prevailed. The British monarchy was set on the course of detachment. The Queen would never cease to be a partisan at heart, but she would be an impartial monarch in outward form.

Although the Prince was determined not to commit himself to a party this did not mean that he was neutral on political questions. In 1845 Peel's uneasy relations with the rank and file of his party came to a crisis when he decided to repeal the Corn Laws. He first resigned, but Russell – now the Whig leader – either through weakness or disinclination declared himself unable to form a government. Peel agreed to come back, and the ensuing Tory revolt, led in the Lords by Derby and in the Commons by Lord George Bentinck and Disraeli, split the party irrevocably. Peel carried the repeal with Whig aid but resigned in summer 1846 after defeat on another question and never held office again. The Prince – and the Queen – strongly supported free trade; they had come to like Peel, and his action putting, as it seemed to them, country before party was just the sort of thing that the Prince admired. One can compare George V and Ramsay MacDonald in 1931. It is curious to note that the Prince's objections to an ex-Prime Minister corresponding confidentially with the Crown were wholly forgotten. He positively encouraged Peel to write to the Queen after his resignation.

It is also curious that Prince Albert, who was such a strong believer in principles, should have failed to see the case for the other side. The Tories had been elected on a programme of protection. From the point of view of Derby, Bentinck, Disraeli and their associates, Peel was the man who was betraying, whereas they were upholding, Tory principles. When the Prince attended in the gallery of the House on a day crucial for Peel's fortunes, thus publicly showing his support, he received an orotund rebuke from Lord George Bentinck in what must be the longest sentence in Hansard – it runs to over 200 words. The Prince never showed himself in the House again.

The new Prime Minister was Lord John Russell. The Prince's relations with him were not satisfactory. Russell was a doctrinaire Whig. He was also remarkably inefficient. Letters were left unanswered for weeks. Replies, when eventually sent, were often wrongly addressed. He frequently cut or forgot appointments. The Prince, methodical to a high degree, was disconcerted. He also deplored Russell's ignorance of 'political economy' and tried to remedy it by sending copies of *The Economist* suitably marked in order to improve the Prime Minister's mind. On one matter, however, the Prince was on Russell's side. He strongly supported the Prime Minister's ecclesiastical appointments, some of which scandalised orthodox Anglican opinion – especially that of Dr Hampden, an extreme low churchman, censured in Oxford for his Bampton lectures, to the Bishopric of Hereford. To the Prince the Oxford High Church movement was a mixture of rubbish and superstition. Cambridge was more sympathetic, but even there he received sharp opposition when he allowed his name to go forward in 1847 for the honorific post of Chancellor. He won by only 117 votes in a poll of 1,791 against Lord Powis, an obscure Tory backwoodsman. It was a clear sign of how controversial a figure he had become – anyway in the eyes of the extreme Right.

Agreement with Russell in ecclesiastical affairs did not lead to any sympathy elsewhere. Russell was shy, awkward and curiously insensitive in social relations. He was indecisive, could vacillate for months on end until some episode reminding him of an archaic Whig principle made him act with reckless impetuousness embarrassing Crown and Cabinet alike. But Russell, though negatively tiresome, was not the Court's main problem. Their real bugbear was the Foreign Secretary (later to be Prime Minister) – Lord Palmerston – who emerged as a positive menace.

Palmerston was born in 1784 and had been almost continuously in office since the age of twenty-two. From 1830 to 1841, with a brief interruption, he had held the Foreign Office. There was no bone of contention between him and the Prince in the last year of that period, but the Prince was still a newcomer and Palmerston an old hand. The royal couple stayed at Broadlands in the summer of 1841 and all was friendly. By 1846 however the Prince had acquired some clear-cut views on foreign policy. These had usually coincided with those of Peel and Aberdeen, and during their time in office relations between Court and Cabinet had been reasonably harmonious. Even then, however, the possibility of conflict existed. The Prince, thanks to his uncle Léopold's tutelage, knew much more about European than British affairs, and he regarded foreign policy as a matter in which the Crown ought to take a very special interest.

There was a further consideration. The Queen and the Prince were related by blood or marriage to most of the crowned heads of Europe at a time when the monarchical principle prevailed almost everywhere. The Court had its own channels of communication, and the Prince who considered English politicians to be insular was determined, as with Lord John Russell on economics, to ensure that they were properly informed. This could be embarrassing when the Court's information flatly contradicted that sent by the relevant ambassador. For example early in 1847 the Court rebuked the Prime Minister – in fact it was a hit at Palmerston – for encouraging the Portuguese liberals against the Queen of Portugal who was married to a Coburg. English influence, Queen Victoria wrote, 'becomes of still greater importance to her when the Sovereigns of that country are her near and dear relations'. Palmerston replied to Russell in a letter meant to be shown to the Queen:

The court [in Lisbon] is guided, I might almost say, governed, by a pedantic and bigotted tutor, by a furious Portuguese Fanatic, by a newspaper Editor, a vulgar man raised suddenly to power and full of low resentments, and by a gambling, drinking, unscrupulous Priest.

Palmerston, an English nationalist relying less on reason than on the instincts developed by a lifetime of experience, brisk, self-confident, anti-intellectual, careless of principle, and too busy to argue every decision, was just the sort of man who was sure to be anathema to the Prince. No one could have been less like Peel, who was grave, thoughtful and meticulous, who invariably kept the Court informed, and who was always ready to meet argument with counter-argument. The conflict, however, was not simply one of personality. There were two further reasons.

First the Court disagreed with the content of Palmerston's policy which differed from that of Peel and Aberdeen. Any description of these differences in a lecture must be an over-simplification. Roughly speaking, Peel and the Court believed in the preservation of the European dynasties and regarded with alarm radical movements, whether social or nationalist, which seemed likely to displace them. This did not mean that they approved of the tyrannical aspects of some monarchical régimes, merely that they regarded revolution as worse and more detrimental to English interests. The Prince firmly believed that kings ought to copy Britain and Belgium, and become 'constitutional', but he also believed that the change should come from within, actuated by the monarch's own convictions. The chances of this happening under the Romanovs, the Habsburgs or the Spanish and Neapolitan Bourbons were of course remote.

Palmerston, reflecting the feeling of most Englishmen, had no particular use for the continental monarchies. Although he was entirely loyal to the British Crown, he would have echoed the Whig sentiments of Lord Holland at the time of the 1815 Restoration – 'When a legitimate King is restored every sprig of Royalty in Europe becomes more insolent and insufferable.' In general he considered liberal movements in Europe favourable to English interests and therefore worthy of a helping hand, and he was well aware that his attitude was highly popular at home.

The second reason for royal antagonism was Palmerston's method. The Court did not, as Lord Clarendon alleged, 'labour under the curious mistake that the Foreign Office is their peculiar department and that they have the right to control, if not to direct the Foreign Policy of England'. This was not so. The Queen and the Prince always accepted a clear Cabinet decision. But the Queen had the right to comment on despatches to her foreign representatives and the right to have her general views on policy considered by the Foreign Secretary, and, if he disagreed, by the Prime Minister and Cabinet. How could she exercise these rights if the Foreign Secretary regularly sent instructions on important matters to British ambassadors without consulting either the Court or the Cabinet? Palmerston was the most powerful figure in a government of ciphers headed by a feeble Prime Minister. As for the Court, he regarded the royal couple as tyros in diplomacy and a source of unnecessary delay. When rebuked, he would apologise, blandly promise not to do it again, and then repeat the offence a few months later.

From 1849 onwards the Queen and the Prince pressed Russell to remove Palmerston from the Foreign Office. The Prime Minister, however, saw that it would be the end of his government, unless he could offer Palmerston a suitable alternative. The only solution he could suggest was to take on the post himself in addition to the premiership, alleviating the extra burden by going to the House of Lords and handing over the leadership of the House of Commons to Palmerston. This was no solution for the Court. Would not Palmerston from his new vantage point soon replace Russell as Prime Minister? And would not such an appointment put the Queen in an impossible position? At this juncture the Prince felt obliged to reveal a dark secret to Russell. He declared that Palmerston while a guest at Windsor Castle had made a brutal attack on Lady Dacre, one of the Queen's Ladies in Waiting. He had entered her bedroom 'at night by stealth... barricaded afterwards the door and would have consummated his fiendish scheme by violence', but for the screams of his victim. Russell agreed that this was 'very bad'. The facts were not as black as the Prince painted them. He did not mention that the episode occurred very early in the Queen's reign before Palmerston was married, and that it was caused by a change in the accommodation at Windsor of which the Foreign Secretary was unaware. The bedroom was normally occupied by a lady to whom Palmerston's entry was highly welcome, and to lock the door was a natural precaution. Such conduct in a guest was very improper, but it could hardly be regarded as a barrier to the premiership ten years later.

Russell did nothing. As long as Palmerston's forays into unauthorised diplomacy were supported by public opinion, as in the cases of Don Pacifico and General Haynau, he was safe, however furious the Court. But late in 1851 he blundered. For reasons still obscure, without consulting Crown or Cabinet, he expressed to the French Ambassador his 'entire approbation' of Louis Napoleon's *coup d'état* on 2 December. This time he was supporting military dictatorship against civil liberty, and Russell, possibly to forestall the Queen, dismissed him on 19 December. The Court was delighted and hoped that the change would lead to an alliance between Russell and the Peelites, the Free Trade Conservative minority which kept green the name of Peel, who had died in 1850. Their joy was short-lived. Before such a junction could occur, Palmerston got his 'tit for tat for Johnny Russell' and in alliance with the Protectionist Conservatives defeated the government on an amendment to the Militia Bill in February 1852. Russell promptly resigned.

The Queen and the Prince now faced the disagreeable prospect of a Protectionist government headed by Lord Derby. He was a notable orator, a distinguished classical scholar, a great race-

horse owner and a man of fashion. He was very clever but somewhat casual and slightly cynical. In the words of Palmerston, which
are a fine example of the pot calling the kettle black, 'Lord Derby
has an offhand and sarcastic way about him which is not the
manner of a courtier.' The Prince saw no alternative; but the
Queen, differing for once on a political issue, reverted to a more
Hanoverian attitude. She feared that the reversal of free trade
would lead to extreme social discontent and encourage French
invasion. She consulted Stockmar on how to avoid Derby.

The Prince was no less devoted than the Queen to the principles
of Peel and he was equally averse to a Protectionist ministry. But
he saw that it would be as unwise to push the Derbyite Conservatives into permanent opposition as it would have been to treat
Peel in the same way eleven years earlier. Ironically in 1852 he
had to overcome the Queen's loyalty to the memory of Peel for
the same reason that he had had to overcome her dislike of him
in 1841 – to put the Crown above the partisan struggle and thus
reaffirm the Coburg concept of monarchy. His advice prevailed,
and the Queen reluctantly sent for Derby.

The royal couple did not, however, give him an easy run. The
Queen told Derby that:

since her accession she had identified herself with a liberal policy which was in
conformity with the wishes of the People...and therefore she felt alarmed lest
it should be considered that she had changed her opinions with the change of
Ministers, and that she hoped therefore that what he would propose would not
be in direct opposition to a liberal policy.

Derby, being in a minority, was in no position to reinstate the
Corn Laws, but he was not going to accept her argument. He
replied that different opinions existed about the wishes of the
people; the constitutional responsibility for its measures rested
with the government; if the country objected, they would be
defeated in Parliament. The Prince hastily reassured him, saying
that the Queen merely wished him to remember her personal
position.

Matters were no easier when Derby came to appointments. At one stage he felt obliged to remark that 'he was sorry he could not offer persons of whom the Queen could say more than "that she did not object to them"'. When it came to Court appointments, the Prince told Derby that they should not be on the verge of bankruptcy and should have moral characters which would bear investigation. Derby asked whether Lord Wilton, an importunate kinsman, could be Master of the Horse. The Prince replied that a man with the nickname of 'the wicked Earl' would not do as head of one of the departments of the Queen's Household. When Derby submitted a list of names for Court appointments from which the Queen could choose, the Prince noted with horror that 'the greater part were the Dandies and Roués of London and the Turf'. He riposted with 'a counter list of some twenty respectable Peers of property', observing that nothing had done more harm to Louis Philippe than the murder of the Duchesse de Praslin by her husband who was attached to his Household. The Prince did, it is true, disclaim the implication that 'Lord Derby's racing friends were capable of such acts'. But the disclaimer can have done little to soften a disagreeable innuendo. Derby did not last long. The general election in the summer of 1852 improved his position but left him still in a minority. The Whigs, Liberals and Peelites combined to defeat Disraeli's autumn budget, and Derby resigned in December.

The situation which he bequeathed was abnormally fluid and obscure. Russell led the largest bloc among the parties which had ousted Derby, but he had not made up his quarrel with Palmerston who had actually abstained in the vote on the budget. The Peelites were headed by Lord Aberdeen. He was regarded by the Court as a sympathetic figure, but he commanded at the most fifty votes in the House. Derby advised the Queen to send for Lord Lansdowne, the elderly *doyen* of the Whig party who had been Chancellor of the Exchequer nearly half a century earlier. The Prince observed that 'constitutionally speaking it did not rest with him [Derby] to give advice and become responsible for it'. In the event the Queen decided to summon Lansdowne and Aberdeen jointly, thus passing over Russell. He probably would not have been able to form a government. But it might have been wiser to let him try. His resentment at not being offered the first place was a source of constant trouble in the ensuing government. Lansdowne was too ill with gout to obey the royal summons, but he backed Aberdeen, on whom the choice fell, to form a coalition government. It was very much a personal selection and by no means an inevitable one. The Court trusted Aberdeen as the exponent of a sound foreign policy and as the custodian of the Peel tradition but there was an obvious difficulty in the Prime Minister heading by far the smaller party in the coalition, especially when he insisted on an equal share in the Cabinet for his followers.

The history of the coalition was largely the history of Russell's perpetual efforts to undermine it. Aberdeen also had the misfortune to deal with the Crimean war – the most serious crisis in Queen Victoria's reign. Aberdeen was strongly pro-Russian, and the Czar Nicholas I's knowledge of this fact caused him to push Russian claims to an extent that he would scarcely have risked if either Russell or Palmerston had been Prime Minister. Unfortunately Aberdeen was not able to control his own Cabinet – a fact which Nicholas could hardly be expected to appreciate. The Prince was anxious for peace but by no means pro-Russian – which did not stop an absurd outbreak of press and public hysteria against him when Palmerston briefly resigned in December 1853. Palmerston soon came back, and the anti-Coburg campaign, whose origins are still a mystery, rapidly died away. If the Court was too mistrustful during Derby's ministry, the Prince and the Queen probably erred the other way during Aberdeen's. He was very much their nominee and protégé, and they were slow to see his weaknesses.

When the scandals of the war forced Aberdeen's resignation, the Court behaved with good sense. First Derby was invited to form a government, and when he failed Russell was asked. He too failed, and the Queen now had no option but to appoint Palmerston himself. Oddly enough, despite the frictions of the past, relations were by no means bad. The Prince closed the special file that he had been keeping since 1848 on Palmerston's iniquities, observing: 'He acts with great prudence and moderation. He receives every support from us in his difficult situation.' Court and Prime Minister had the same objective – an early and victorious end to the war. This occurred in the spring of 1856. Less than a year later, defeated on his Chinese policy, Palmerston obtained a dissolution and increased his majority, only to crash the following year; the cause for the second time was an attempt to placate Louis Napoleon who had barely escaped assassination from a bomb made in England. But his not unreasonable request to have the law on conspiracy to murder tightened up met with a wave of anti-French sentiment.

The Crown now had to have Derby again. Relations with him were better than before, but the Prince continued to have misgivings:

We have great difficulties [he wrote to King Léopold] with the question of reform. The irresponsibility of Derby and the complete lack of character and untruthfulness of Disraeli put all the weapons in the hands of the Democrats, for they undermine the confidence of the moderates of all parties.

It is curious that the Prince's opinion of both Disraeli and Gladstone was so different from the Queen's in her later life. As everyone knows she came to be devoted to Disraeli and to detest Gladstone. The Prince could see no merit at all in Disraeli and pronounced that he 'had not one single element of a gentleman in his composition'. Gladstone, however, apart from his High Church opinions, which the Prince found incomprehensible, appeared to him as the true heir of Peel. The Prince strongly approved of his sincerity and seriousness.

The second Derby minority government lasted little longer than the first – some sixteen months. The Court's relations with Derby were better than before. He was readily granted a dissolution in 1859 after his defeat on a new Reform Bill. The reason for this improvement was not positive sympathy. It was dislike of the opposition. The Italian crisis was the great question of Europe. The Court was pro-Austrian. The Whig opposition – Palmerston and Russell – were hostile and supported Italian nationalism. Derby's attitude was nearer to that of the Court. But he lost the election and resigned. The Queen showed her appreciation by giving him the Garter. She offered the premiership to Lord Granville hoping that Palmerston and Russell – 'the two terrible old men', as she called them – would serve under him. The plan did not work, and Palmerston again became Prime Minister with Lord John as Foreign Secretary.

The Prince died two and a half years later in December 1861 at the age of forty-two. His last political act was to suggest amendments to a Foreign Office despatch to the American Government on the Trent affair; these were accepted and may well have averted, if not war, at least a breach of relations with very serious implications for the future.

Disraeli, who was quite unaware of the Prince's adverse opinion of him, wrote:

With Prince Albert we have buried our sovereign. This German Prince has governed England for twenty-one years with a wisdom and energy such as none of our Kings have ever shown...If he had outlived our 'old stagers' he would have given us, while retaining our constitutional guarantees, the blessings of absolute government.

This, like some other pronouncements by Disraeli, is highly misleading. It was made more so by Lytton Strachey whose life of Queen Victoria coloured the picture of the Prince for a whole generation of readers and who quoted it without the qualification about 'constitutional guarantees'. The Prince might perhaps have acquired even more influence with the passage of time. On the other hand, events from 1867 onwards – the year of the Second Reform Act – operated so as to limit the exercise of the royal prerogative. The period from 1840 to the Prince's death was one of general elections that were mostly indecisive (1841 was an exception) and of parliaments with no clear party majority. The general election of 1868, for whatever reason, inaugurated a period of definite results which gave less scope for the Crown's intervention.

In any case the last thing that the Prince favoured was an authoritarian monarchy. He was mindful of the dignity and importance of the Crown and he believed that it had an active part to play, but he always thought in terms of a limited constitutional monarchy, never in terms of one that 'would have given us the blessings of absolute government'. His attitude towards the efforts to turn the German Confederation into a unified state must be seen in this light. He was sometimes criticised for being too much in favour of the Coburgs and of German unification. In fact he never subordinated British interests to either his family or his national sentiments. A liberal Germany united under the rule of a liberal King of Prussia was in his lifetime a perfectly reasonable aspiration and would have been advantageous to the balance of power in Europe. Bismarck was not appointed till 1862, a year after the Prince's death. It is safe to assume that he would not have approved of the authoritarian régime which eventually resulted from that fateful decision. It is also safe to assume that he could have done very little to prevent it or to modify its consequences.

It is true that the Prince regarded himself as essentially German and thought of England as his adopted country, not really as his own. It is hard to blame him for that, but it goes some of the way to account for his undoubted unpopularity, which hindered him in his task. Not that foreigners were necessarily disliked by the English upper class. The success of Count D'Orsay is evidence on that point. But a foreign Prince who palpably regarded the English aristocracy as a set of dissolute rakes, who invariably spoke German with the Queen, and who observed that 'no tailor in England can make a coat' was not likely to endear himself to the sort of men who governed England in the 1840s and 1850s. They were slightly mollified when it became known that he was an excellent rider to hounds and a first-class shot. But the effect of his prowess with the gun was neutralised by his chosen dress – a black velvet jacket and long scarlet leather boots – and his insistence on interrupting the sport to eat a hot luncheon, cold being the invariable custom of the day. He never joined a club, though it would have been regarded as perfectly natural for him to be a member of, say, White's; and he made no friendships, unlike the Queen, who was on easy and familiar terms with several members of the aristocracy. To cap all this, he disliked the hallowed English custom of the men remaining at the dinner table while the port decanter circulated, and he was accustomed when he was host to rejoin the ladies a quarter of an hour before the rest of the party, and to sing duets with the Queen.

Besides these social disadvantages, the Prince acquired unpopularity by pitching his own claims too high. He once declared that he was not only the Queen's 'sole confidential adviser in politics' and 'the private secretary of the sovereign' but also 'her permanent minister'. Mr Le May after quoting this passage in his admirable book, *The Victorian Constitution,* rightly observes 'It was the last of these capacities which no politician could concede to the Prince...The Prince could not be a "minister" for the same reason that he could not be Commander-in-Chief – because he could not be dismissed.' The logic of the claim would have entailed the Prince actually sitting in at Cabinet meetings – a rôle which no sovereign or consort had played in England since the reign of George I.

The Prince and the Queen (inspired by the Prince) were apt to nag at their ministers, especially the Prime Minister. The sheer time involved in correspondence was a serious matter for busy men. Peel in 1845 complained that the general burden on the Prime Minister had become intolerable while Parliament was sitting, and second in a long list of indispensable duties he put the need to 'keep up constant communication with the Queen *and the Prince*' – the last three words being underlined for emphasis. The Prince's flow of letters was quite deliberate. 'I had often heard it stated', he wrote, '...that the Sovereign could not interfere with the Government...Now I differed completely from that doctrine. I held the Sovereign to have an immense moral responsibility upon his shoulders with regard to his government and the duty to watch and control it.' Evidently constitutional monarchy as seen by the Prince and the Queen was by no means the same as it became a century later.

Nevertheless there had been a real change between 1840 and 1861. The Prince's influence had helped to remove the Crown from party politics. Neither the Prince nor the Queen had become neutral about political questions in the wider sense of the word 'political', and the Prince was not always consistent in his attitude, for example towards Melbourne and Peel corresponding as ex-Prime Ministers with the Queen. But the monarchy under his conscientious and carefully considered counsel had silently moved into a new era. Circumstances and events outside his control were pushing in the same direction, but a different person advising the Queen might have produced frictions, obstacles and difficulties which could have damaged, possibly even prevented altogether, the development of the monarchy as we now know it.

If, as I believe, the history of the British Crown has been one of the great success-stories of the last hundred years, and if it remains one of the few institutions which have not in recent times come under serious, as opposed to merely frivolous or spiteful criticism, the Prince Consort deserves a substantial share of the credit. The exact effect of personality upon politics is a subject for infinite debate. I would merely argue that, but for the Prince, things might have developed very differently, and that it was in his relations with successive Prime Ministers that he made his greatest contribution to the constitutional monarchy which Britain enjoys today.

PRINCE ALBERT AND THE ARTS AND SCIENCES

ASA BRIGGS

IN A LITTLE BOOK of sermons on *The Late Prince Consort: Reminiscences of his Life and Character*, published soon after his death and very quickly selling twenty thousand copies, the Rev. J. H. Wilson devoted his first sermon to what he called 'aesthetics'. Beginning with the text that 'all flesh is grass and all the goodliness thereof is as the flower of the field', Wilson went on to compare beauty and fragrance in nature with beauty and fragrance in what he called 'the moral world' – 'in the growth of virtue, the cultivation of taste and of science, the courtesies of life and the promotion of the fine arts'. 'And', he declared, 'just as the humblest subject, like the mountain daisy, may be radiant with beauty in the cottage of the poor, so the most exalted citizen, like the rose of Sharon, may be fragrant in the garden of the Queen.'

This was priestly rhetoric about royalty – with echoes of the priestly rhetoric of the past. Yet seldom, if ever, in the past – or at least in Britain's past – and never since would it have been possible to treat, as Wilson did in 1861, the cultivation of both science and the arts as a beautiful and fragrant activity in the 'moral world'. George IV had certainly cultivated the arts as lavish patron, but there was some doubt about his place in the moral world. Charles II more than a century before had not been indifferent to the development of science, but there was doubt

51

about his place in the moral world also. Concerning Albert's place in that world there has never been any doubt: he was 'Albert the good'. Nor has there been any doubt either about his genuine and deep interest both in science and the arts – not to speak of music, which satisfied him emotionally – or of his own sense that they were all intimately related with morality at a genuine and deep level.

'Science', he proclaimed, at an elaborate banquet held at the Mansion House in March 1850, fourteen months before the opening of the Great Exhibition, 'discovers...laws of power, motion and transformation; industry applies them to the raw matter which the earth yields us in abundance but which becomes valuable only by knowledge.' Art 'elevates', teaching us 'the immovable laws of beauty and symmetry' and gives to our products 'forms in accordance with them'. Music, to be represented at the opening ceremonies of the Great Exhibition by Handel's *Hallelujah Chorus*, with organ, 200 instruments and 600 voices and the War March of the Priests from *Athalie*, consoles or inspires. Religion supports morality; the Archbishop of Canterbury's prayer at the opening acknowledged that the Lord above had 'multiplied on us blessings which Thou mightest most justly have withheld', but Albert's own statement on religion and morality in his Mansion House speech had a somewhat different dimension. Like the Archbishop, he claimed that 'the first impression which the view of this vast collection will produce upon the spectator will be that of devout thankfulness to the Almighty for the blessings which He has bestowed upon us here below'. Yet Albert went further. Such blessings, he concluded, could only be realised 'in proportion to the help which we are prepared to render each other; therefore, only by peace, love and ready assistance not only between individuals but between the nations of the earth'.

Significantly, Wilson's second sermon, reflecting on the theme of Albert's life and work, was called 'social economics'. Albert 'would reason by analogy', Wilson stated, 'and argue on the principle that, as the ocean is composed of globules of water, the sunbeam of particles of light, and the earth of atoms of matter, each one cohesive and having affinity for every other, society, in order to be harmonious, must also have its units in perspective; and hence his intense desire for the thorough practical cultivation of the *individual* mind'.

In such a vision – and it is not improper to call it such – Albert felt that analogy acquired the force of law. He had a strong sense too of the specificity of his own time and of the forces making for development within it. The 'peculiar textures' of the nineteenth century were pointing towards new unities, above all 'the realisation of the unity of mankind'. Distance was being annihilated, the division of labour, 'the moving power of civilisation', was being extended to all branches of science, industry and art, and knowledge was becoming open, not esoteric. 'So man is approaching a more complete fulfilment of that great and sacred wisdom which he has to perform in this world. His reason being created of the image of God, he has to use it to discover the laws by which the Almighty governs His creation, and by making these laws his standard of action, to conquer nature to his use, himself a divine instrument.'

For Albert this was more than rhetoric. When the Great Exhibition opened in May 1851 – a scene which, in the Queen's words, could 'never be effaced from my memory' or ever would be 'from that of anyone who witnessed it' – Albert's name, she felt, had already been 'immortalised'. 'Most justly may the Prince be proud of today', wrote Edward Kater, who had been seated opposite the throne. 'It seemed more like the realisation of the thoughts of the poet or painter, or some delightful fairy tale.' Even Lord John Russell, the Prime Minister, caught a glimpse of Albert's vision. 'The wonders of Art and Industry will be the most celebrated among philosophers and men of science', he told the Queen, 'as well as among manufacturers and the great mass of the working people', although he added too – as did many visitors from Continental Europe – that what was 'perhaps the most gratifying to a politician' was 'the general conduct of the multitudes assembled'. At the end of the Exhibition Russell wrote again of 'the grandeur of the conception' as well as 'the zeal, invention, and talent displayed in the exhibition' and 'the perfect order maintained from the first day to the last'.

Albert's vision was philosophical rather than magical or political. It was reflected in the mottoes in the Exhibition Catalogue which he chose personally as much as in the objects on display. The mottoes included both Biblical texts of the kind Wilson or the Archbishop of Canterbury would have chosen, 'The Earth is the Lord's and all that therein is', for example, and texts with a distinctive nineteenth-century ring, one written by Albert himself, 'The progress of the human race resulting from the labour of all men ought to be the final object of the exertion of each individual. In promoting this end, we are carrying out the will of the Great and Blessed God'.

This philosophical vision was not reflected, however, in the system of classification of objects. Albert was always drawn to classification. Yet the extremely simple classification of objects into three sections which he proposed – the raw materials of industry, the manufactures made from them and the art used to adorn them – was replaced by a more complicated scheme of Lyon Playfair's which appealed to manufacturers more than to philosophers. Manufacturers were to be organised through eight main groups – metallurgy; chemical manufactures; vitreous ceramic manufactures; textiles; organic manufactures; engineering and machinery; architecture, fine arts and music; and agriculture and horticulture – and objects were to be divided into twenty-eight classes, each subdivided into sections, representing distinct industries. 'High art' had deliberately been left out of the plan, although it came in via sculpture, which could involve foundry work and the application of machines.

Writers on the Exhibition then and since have pointed to the replacement of the system of classification as reflecting the difference between the systematically philosophical German mind and the practical, businesslike British mind: as Yvonne ffrench put it simply in her book on *The Great Exhibition*, published in 1950 on the eve of the 1951 Festival of Britain, 'the German approach to the problem relied too much upon an intellectual solution; too little on simplicity. It tended to classify, to generalise, to postulate.' This was putting it too simply, for if Albert's plan was deemed impracticable, it certainly was not on account of its lack of simplicity, nor because of its tendency to classify. What seemed to be at stake was the English demand for a kind of Gradgrind factual commonsense. The French were eventually won over to Playfair's scheme, Playfair stated, after a supremely practical test on how to classify the French Commissioner's massive walking stick. Playfair placed it at once in one of his subsections, 'objects for personal use': after long deliberation the French Commissioner placed it under a French subsection, 'machines for the production of direct motion'. 'He laughed heartily', Playfair wrote, 'and agreed to work under the English classification.'

There is rather more to the matter than this. Albert's philosophy, which lay behind his simple system of classification, did not reflect what had actually happened to British industry in the course of the rapid industrialisation which had followed Watt's invention of his steam engine. It was not the case, as his vision suggested, that 'science discovers laws of power, motion and transformation' and 'industry applies them'. The invention of the steam engine preceded the discovery of the laws of thermodynamics. Indeed, in 1851 British industry as a whole was based on empiricism far more than on science. The difference between Britain and Germany in this connection was to be made much of later in the nineteenth century after industrialisation had proceeded further. Playfair, who was himself a scientist and had worked in industry, realised more clearly than Albert in 1851 how

British manufacturers actually operated and thought of their operations: later in the century, as a Liberal Member of Parliament, he was strongly to support the improvement of British technical education and to refer to German superiority in this field. Whether or not Playfair – or Albert – knew in 1851 of the Prussian civil servant Alexander von Minotoli's efforts during the 1830s and 1840s to relate art to science, particularly through an industrial museum, is not clear.

In retrospect, we can see that there was less science than energy and ingenuity behind the great Victorian collection assembled in the Crystal Palace, a collection which above all else inspired wonder and awe rather than wisdom and understanding. Some of the critics of the Exhibition had a very different vision from that of Albert even concerning the building. 'The quantity of bodily industry which the Crystal Palace expresses', wrote Ruskin, of the building itself, 'is very great. So far it is good. The quantity of thought it expresses is, I suppose, a single and admirable thought...probably not a bit brighter than thousands of thoughts which pass through (its designer Paxton's) active and intelligent brain every hour – that it might be possible to build a greenhouse larger than ever greenhouse was built before.' As for the objects, it remains interesting to turn to Gottfried Semper's *Wissenschaft, Industrie und Kunst*, published in Brunswick in 1852, and written possibly at Albert's invitation: 'only in products in which the seriousness of their use does not allow anything unnecessary, that is in coaches, weapons, medical instruments etc. one can occasionally see a sounder way of decorating and improving form'.

The Queen was delighted in a spontaneous and uncomplicated way both with the cornucopia of objects on display and with many of the individual objects, not discriminating between raw materials and finished products, arts and sciences or British and foreign: thus, she could write of the French Court that 'the taste and execution are quite unequalled and gave one a wish to buy all one saw' and more generally (and as eloquently as Andrew Ure, 'philosopher of manufactures', satirised by Marx) of beautiful cotton machines which accomplished 'in a few instants' what 'used to be done by hand and take months'. Yet Henry Cole, who had worked closely with Albert in every stage of the preparations for the Exhibition, was less easily impressed either by the design or display or by the speed of production. Dickens might associate Cole with the Gradgrind School in *Hard Times* (without actually naming him), but it was members of the so-called Cole group who attacked in *The Times* 'the sins committed against good taste' and 'the vulgarities of our manufactures' and tried to set standards. Richard Redgrave, editor of *The Journal of Design and Manufactures*, the first number of which in March 1849 had been dedicated to Albert, complained bitterly of 'the absence of any fixed principle in ornamental design' in the Exhibition. 'It will be readily allowed', he wrote in his official *Supplementary Report on Design*, that 'the mass of ornament applied to the works...' exhibited was 'meretricious'. The same point was made in his statement of 1853 *On The Necessity of Principles in Teaching Design*. Meanwhile, R. N. Warnum's *The Exhibition is a Lesson in Taste* had comprehensively described 'the taste of the producers in general' as 'uneducated'.

We can see, therefore, that honest though Albert's vision was, there could be a gulf between banquet speeches and contemporary criticism, a gulf which could only be bridged, if at all, through education. Yet when we turn from words to objects, we see some of the difficulties even in starting the operation. Take the four-feet-high vase, with square mounted pedestal and crowned by a statuette of Albert himself, and exhibited by Elkington, the Birmingham firm which had pioneered silver electroplating. It was called *The Triumph of Science* and was designed and modelled by William Beattie. There were four other statuettes at each corner – one of Newton, standing for Astronomy; one of Shakespeare, standing for Poetry – a sign that the arts and sciences

57

could often be put together at this time, not only by Albert; one of Bacon, standing for Philosophy – a reminder that Baconian philosophy, or at least one version of it, was very close to the core of Albert's own philosophy; and one of James Watt, standing for Mechanics. At the base of the vase were two even more symbolic figures of Man and Woman. Electroplating was one of the new technical triumphs of the day – hailed by the Queen herself – but the style of this remarkable object, which Nikolaus Pevsner identifies as 'dixhuitième if anything', was described in the catalogue as 'Elizabethan'. For all the symbolism and the fantasy, the reliefs on the side of the square between the statuettes were described as 'practical operations of Science and Art', each with capital letters. The ambiguities of taste in 1851 are plain enough in the Queen's comment in her *Journal* for 12 July – 'The taste of some of the plate and jewellery is beautiful: none struck us so much, as likely to be useful for the taste of the country, as Elkington's beautiful specimens of electroplate.' Did she include Albert in the royal 'us'? I believe that she did.

On that very same day some of the economic and social ambiguities of 1851 were apparent also. The royal visitors studied a model cottage for four families, commissioned by Albert himself and erected not far from the Crystal Palace in the grounds of Knightsbridge Cavalry Barracks. Their host was the great Evangelical philanthropist, Lord Shaftesbury. Construction of the cottage, which looks attractive in the drawings, was entirely in hollow brick, no timber was used for floor or ceilings, and access was by a central open staircase. Here again was a visible token of Albert's belief in social economy, already demonstrated in his Presidency of the Society for Improving the Conditions of the Working Classes, set up in 1844, the year of Engels's *Condition of the Working Class*, and in a group of Albert Dwellings in Spitalfields built in 1848, the year of Europe's revolutions. Charles Dickens, who did not much like the Exhibition or the objects on display there, hailed Albert's initiative. Yet when the basic design of the cottage was used on a far larger scale in tenement blocks during the 1860s by the Improved Industrial Dwellings Company and the Peabody Trust, it can scarcely be said to have been aesthetically or socially successful.

The social ambiguities of 1851 are revealed, too, in *Punch*'s demand – and what a magnificent satirical source the *Punch* of this time is – for 'a real exposition of the industrious' alongside the exposition of industry: 'in a glass hive we ought to show the bees at work. However, as needlewomen cannot be starved, nor tailors "sweated", nor miners blown up amongst a multitude of peoples with any degree of safety, it is suggested that paintings of our various artisans, labouring in their usual vocations, should accompany the display of substances and fabrics which we owe to the labours and ingenuity of the respective classes. Pictorial art might thus be brought to make appropriate contributions to the world's bazaar. Shall we ostentatiously show off all manner of articles of comfort and luxury and be ashamed to disdain the condition of those whom we have to thank for them?'

Whatever else might be said in 1851, there could be no doubt about Albert's own capacity for work. 'I am at present more dead than alive from overwork', he wrote to the Dowager Duchess of Coburg two weeks before the Exhibition opened; while according to the Queen he was 'terribly fagged' – a vivid phrase – on the day before the opening. Richard Cobden, who served as a Commissioner, described him plainly as 'a working man'. His interest in 'real' physical work – skilled and unskilled – was exceptional, as was his interest in detail. On visits to the Exhibition before the opening he would watch carefully workmen engaged in all the intricate processes of drilling, punching and boring, and he was just as interested in materials as in structures – checking on rubble, for instance, and carefully noting Colonel Reid's testing of wind pressure and of fire precautions.

Albert had vision, but he was no dreaming visionary. Sir Robert Peel, whom he greatly admired and who died – to Albert's great sadness and consternation – in the difficult year before the Exhibition opened, put him in touch with many supremely practical scientists like Playfair. It was Playfair, indeed, who, at Peel's suggestion, discussed with Albert the Prince's proposed new method of filtration for sewage 'so as to keep back the fertile ingredients and allow the effluent water to pass away'. One would be tempted to consider such a sanitary preoccupation as being as far removed as possible from the art and science of the Crystal Palace were it not for the fact that the sanitary idea of the 1840s was one of the key ideas of the time – possessed itself of both urgency and 'grandeur of conception'. Albert and others like him felt that in seeking to pursue it they were getting behind Fate itself to the saving of wasted life as well as of waste products.

To place Albert's views on the relationship between science and art in perspective, it is necessary to look back rather more generally not only at 1851 but at the 1840s, the troubled decade which preceded the Great Exhibition, a decade not of proclaimed social harmony but of obvious social conflict. Albert, married in 1840, arrived in Britain at a time of both political and economic uncertainty, and his relationship with the Conservative Sir Robert Peel, who became Prime Minister in 1841, was as important in establishing his confidence as Prince – though in a quite different way – as Victoria's much-discussed relationship with the Whig Lord Melbourne was in establishing her confidence as Queen. Peel was thirty-one years older than Albert, about the essential span of a generation, and he found the Prince 'one of the most extraordinary young men' he had met. He was impressed by both his seriousness and his concern. Age relationships matter immensely in the whole of the subsequent story, as they mattered immensely, as J. M. Young has shown us, in Victorian culture as a whole.

Before Peel took office, Albert was writing to his mother how the general election, which Peel won, was 'emptying purses, setting families by the ears, demoralising the lower classes, and perverting many of the upper, whose character wants strength to keep them straight'. He never substantially changed his opinion of many members of the English aristocracy – Peel, 'the spinning Jenny', often ill-at-ease in aristocratic circles, very obviously did not belong to this group – but as his attention very soon shifted from elections to science and the arts and to what was usually called 'the condition of England question', he looked beyond the immediate electoral issues to more basic elements in the society and the culture. Like Peel himself, who built up a superb private art collection and cultivated men of science like de la Bêche and Playfair, he saw from the start that there were important interrelationships between science, art and the social economy. There were always men of merit who were willing to work with him, even though one zealous free trader, Henry Dunckley, who greatly admired Cobden, called him a 'most kind, eccentric, infallible and unfathomable German'.

It was Peel who invited him to undertake his first public task as Prince – to serve at the head of a Royal Commission, of which Charles Eastlake was secretary, 'to inquire whether advantage might not be taken of the rebuilding of the Houses of Parliament to promote and encourage the Fine Arts in the United Kingdom'. As Sir Theodore Martin remarked in his biography of Albert, 'no better introduction into English public life could have been desired for the Prince'. The subject of the inquiry, besides being peculiarly congenial to his tastes, was one in which he was thoroughly at home. The Commission, constituted wholly without reference to party, included men of the first distinction in politics, art and literature; and while in the collision of such minds the Prince could not fail to acquire 'knowledge of the character of the most influential men in England' and 'insight into English ways of thinking and transacting business', he was able at the same time to let his own 'high qualities be seen'.

Appropriately, Albert's letter of acceptance to Peel is the first letter he wrote in English which is quoted by Martin. Yet perhaps equally appropriately it begins with a reference to the *Nibelun-*

genlied in which Peel had expressed interest when they first met. Indeed, the Prince sent Peel a copy to look at with illustrations by Bendemann and Hübner and 'fine specimens of the school of Düsseldorf'. It is not certain whether or not they discussed also the Prince's visit to Florence (and Rome) in 1839, an important event in his life and his education, although he certainly discussed this with the Queen who recalled after his death how delighted he had been with the Pitti Palace. His education in Germany had been very different from that of a nineteenth-century English schoolboy – with less classics and more history, music and natural sciences. We know little of specific influences on him either at school or university (of Immanuel Fichte and August von Schlegel, for example, two of his professors at Bonn). He probably learnt his habits of industry, however, before he arrived in England: as Martin put it, while still a schoolboy, Albert was 'such a hard reading man as men of our universities might almost have shrunk from', with many of his studies 'self-imposed' and directly related to 'accomplishments which seem to embellish and adorn life'.

His own 'high qualities', the product of aptitude, temperament and education, were plain to see in 1841, when he took up his chairmanship of the Royal Commission. He startled his fellow members by proving that in what Lady Eastlake years later called 'neutral ground in public matters on which a royal individual may safely tread' he already had strong ideas of his own. Queen Victoria traced his tastes back to his father, Ernest I: in fact, as John Steegman and Winslow Ames have shown, they had more than one source of inspiration. His tact was remarkable in itself. German artists, he wisely pointed out, need not be employed to produce frescoes, though interest in frescoes was a reflection of the influence which German art was then exerting in England: in all that related to 'practical dexterity', he claimed, the English were 'particularly skilful': among the several instances he gave was 'even to the varnish on coaches, it is surprising how much more perfect the English practice is than that one sees on the Continent'. 'There are two great auxiliaries in this country', Albert went on, 'which seldom fail to promote the success of any scheme – fashion and a high example.' 'Fashion we know is all in all in England, and if the Court – I mean the Queen and myself – set the example hereafter by having works of this kind done (i.e. frescoes), the same taste will extend itself to worthy individuals. The English country seats, which are the most beautiful in the world, would acquire additional effect from the introduction of such a style of decoration, and with such occupation the school would never languish and would at least have time to develop itself fully.'

This statement, based on imperfect knowledge of English society and cultures, greatly appealed to Eastlake, himself a Peel protégé, who was forty-eight years old, twenty-six years older than the Prince and five years younger than Peel. He had established his reputation as a painter, but by the time that he became President of the Royal Academy in 1850 that particular reputation belonged to the past. Years before then and afterwards his main reputation was as an art director. He became Secretary to the National Gallery in 1843 and Director in 1855, and supported by his wife, the remarkable Elizabeth, a force in her own right – and by Albert and the Queen – he did much to set the official taste of mid-Victorian England. He died four years after Albert in 1865 at Pisa – in the same year as Lord Palmerston, the Prime Minister, a real break which some historians have seen as the effective end of the mid-Victorian years.

The mid-Victorian years look very different from the different vantage points from which we can view them or choose to view them. In the light of what came later they seemed to be years of compromise: in the light of what came before they seemed to be years of harmony. They were certainly to be far more comfortable than most critics and prophets had anticipated when Albert became Chairman of the Royal Commission. The Great Exhibition is usually taken as being the great landmark dividing years of comfort – and compromise – based on what Professor Burn called 'equipoise' from the years of conflict which had preceded them. Yet it is impossible to understand the mid-Victorian period without understanding the early-Victorian, for many of the same forces continued to operate. One of them was the force of the market which Albert left out of his statement of 1841 concerning the forces which 'promoted the success of any scheme': he was still caught up in a theory of patronage and of diffusion of taste through patronage. Moreover, he talked of one 'taste' rather than many at a time when taste was no longer taken for granted.

Market forces were already influencing both discussions about taste and education in 'taste'. As early as 1835 in an essay called 'How to observe', Eastlake himself had asked – if not answered – the question whether the arts should be considered as possessing utility as well as beauty and the spiritual values associated with it, and as early as 1840 Francis Palgrave in an article in the *Quarterly Review* on 'The Results of Machinery' had asked another leading question whether the influence of new inventions, like the steam engine, the steel plate and the daguerrotype would be good or bad.

Eastlake's uncertainties in 1835 are brought out in his statement that 'in the hands of English landscape painters the useful capabilities of art, however extensively cultivated, have never been suffered to supersede its more tasteful attributes'. It was a statement which would have been couched differently in both 1841 and 1851. Likewise, Palgrave's certainties were open to question by the latter date. His view that there would be a 'permanent glut of pseudo art' was shared even then by some writers, like Ruskin, as it has been echoed by historians, yet his prophecy that 'art can never again take root in the affections of mankind' proved plainly wrong. Eastlake could have told him this as early as 1843, when an exhibition of cartoons in Westminster Hall which he had arranged was a great popular success. 'I abridged the Catalogue to a penny size for the millions', he wrote to Albert, 'but many of the most wretchedly dressed people prefer the six-penny one with the quotations...All the workmen of the Houses of Parliament go in, but chiefly in the evening, because, being as white as millers, they have themselves the discretion to time their visit.' The Exhibition served the task of 'humanising the people', but in Eastlake's opinion it strongly proved also 'the love of the lower orders for pictures'.

We can see now with the benefit of hindsight that conflicts about taste, including the dominating argument about Classical and Gothic, which were so strident during the 1840s as the rule of taste was undermined both by market and by cultural forces, were to end eventually in a welter of mid-Victorian compromises – in a blend of styles, often 'freely treated', to use the contemporary jargon, rather than in the imposition of one single style, and Winslow Ames has suggested that we should choose the 1862 Exhibition rather than the first Exhibition of 1851 as the 'high Victorian' landmark event, bringing to a close the 'battle of style'. What we should also see is that the Victorians of all classes preferred it to begin and end that way. The undermining of the rule of taste started with a conscious revolt against previous Georgian taste, which began to seem monolithic and monotonous. The death in 1837 of Sir John Soane, 'the last of the great architect disciplinarians', was a symbolic event in the story, co-incidentally occurring as it did in the same year as Victoria came to the throne. Thereafter Georgian attitudes towards elegance, correctness and balance were challenged in architecture, crafts and the arts themselves, through struggle before there was compromise. The crescents of Bath seemed monotonous, Chippendale furniture and Adam fireplaces dull, and eighteenth-century painting both of people and of landscapes inferior to nineteenth-century painting. It was increasingly fashionable to move back in time before the eighteenth century to earlier centuries, 'olden times', particularly, perhaps, the thirteenth. In 1847 *Punch* was to write that if cultures were to be judged by posterity in terms of their monuments and works of art 'we shall be treated as people who live in the middle ages, for everything around us partakes of the medieval character'.

Now Albert did not live in the middle ages, and he accepted the fact – partly through his growing interest in science and technology which he does not appear to have had when he came to England – that England was above all an industrial country. This led him away from his early emphasis on patronage to a more profound appreciation of the economic, social and cultural forces at work in a rapidly changing country. His increasingly varied public activities after 1841 directed his thoughts and imagination, in relation to the arts, in a more sharply focussed way. 'History, literature, science and art seemed to have lent their stores to form the mind of the prince', wrote an English artist in 1847, describing both Albert and the Queen as 'an example to the age'. Yet Albert recognised specialisation as one facet of his age, a facet to which he referred at the 1850 Mansion House dinner. 'To an architect he could talk as an architect', wrote the great engineer Robert Rawlinson in 1846, 'to an engineer as an engineer, to a painter as a painter, to a sculptor as a sculptor, to a chemist as a chemist, and so through all the branches of Engineering, Architecture, Art and Science.' But it was not only to individuals that he could talk: increasingly he became involved with institutions.

One of them was a prestigious but traditionalist institution, Cambridge University, of which he became Chancellor in 1847, after an awkward and disturbing contested election, the first and last election, of course, in his princely career: in the largest poll ever known in the history of the university, 1,791, he secured a majority of 117 against an aristocratic opponent. In an ode written for the occasion by the aged poet Wordsworth – the young poet Tennyson was unwilling to produce one – Albert was apostrophised as follows:

> Prince, in these collegiate bowers
> Where science, leagued with holier truth,
> Guards the sacred heart of youth,
> Solemn monitors are ours.

Albert, however, did not need 'solemn monitors', particularly to watch over science. As an old Cambridge man, Wordsworth knew more then of Cambridge than of the Prince, but the Prince knew far more about science and the temper of his time. As the historian of the University, D. A. Winstanley, has written, Albert's installation was 'something more than a ceremonial and festive occasion' worthy of a Wordsworth ode. 'He entered upon his office with a far higher conception of its duties than any of his predecessors.' And in the movement for university reform, led from outside Cambridge and Oxford, he not only had extremely sensible things to say about the place of the sciences in a university and the reform of teaching and examinations generally, but set out to save the University from itself while keeping it free from government. Winstanley's verdict is that while his was always a difficult task 'he succeeded in accomplishing it'.

A second institution with which Albert was perhaps in greater sympathy and where there was seldom any doubt of his success was the Royal Society for the Encouragement of Arts, Manufactures and Commerce, of which he became President in 1845, succeeding his uncle, the Duke of Sussex. No change of royal patronage could have been more decisive. It was through this body that the idea of the Great Exhibition took shape during the late 1840s, and it was through his association with it that Albert was brought into contact with a more remarkable nineteenth-century Englishman than any of his Cambridge Vice-Chancellors, Henry Cole, a man of extraordinary sensitivity and energy, who has rightly been described as 'a Prince Consort in miniature'. Thackeray, who wrote an ode on the Great Exhibition, was a close friend, and he would have fully approved – despite his distaste for such things – of the motto on the title-page of Cole's biography, *Fifty Years of Public Work* – 'Whatsoever thy hand findeth to do, do it with thy might.'

Cole's background and career were completely different from those of the Prince. Born in 1808, and surviving the Prince by twenty-one years, Cole had already made his mark – before he was consulted by the Society of Arts in 1845 in the first year of Albert's Presidency – first as an Assistant Keeper of the Public Record Office, in the establishment of which he had played an important part behind the scenes, and second as secretary of the militant voluntary organisation set up to crusade for the penny post in 1838, during which he had emerged into public view – a versatile and ambitious (some said too ambitious) man with a remarkable and sure command of both the verbal and the visual. In 1845, when he won a prize himself for the design of 'a complete tea set' in a Society of Arts competition, about which he had been a consultant, he coined the memorable term 'art manufactures', meaning fine art applied to mechanical production: it is a term which has made its way into history through such influential twentieth-century books as Siegfried Giedion's *The Machine Takes Command*, and through contemporary institutions like the Design Council. There were more immediate implications, however. Albert, who saw an exhibition of the successful entries, inspected the tea service, found it to be entirely his taste, and commissioned other articles from Cole. The foreign prince, who popularised the Christmas tree, had joined forces with the man who invented the Christmas card. The two men worked hard together, thereafter, on the scheme for an exhibition on a far bigger scale than those of 1845 or 1847, and it was on Albert's initiative and insistence that the idea took shape that it should be an exhibition of 'all the nations', not merely a display of British products. The two men agreed also that 'the cost of the Exhibition should be provided by voluntary subscriptions and not by the general taxation of the state', and this was an important turning point in the Prince's English education. Through this agreement, he was pulled still further from the patronage system into closer contact with opinion (and tastes) developing from below, not all of them sympathetic to the idea of a Great Exhibition. Indeed, Albert was to meet just as active and at times just as prejudiced national opposition between 1849 and 1851 as he had met from senior members of Cambridge University.

It was Cole's own considered opinion that no one but the Prince could have overcome all the noisy and usually ill-informed opposition and triumphed over all the practical difficulties concerning site, building, finance, classification and transport and presentation of objects, and that his success rested on a combination of personal qualities and advantages of princely rank – what his admirers called 'statesmanship'. He had to make many sacrifices also – above all of time. He had to sacrifice some of his own ideas also – not only his own scheme of classification, but the narrowing of the range of exhibits in the 'Fine Art' sections: oil paintings, water colours, drawings, engravings and, not least, frescoes were all excluded. This was to be above all an Exhibition of Industry. And so, despite the presence of one giant sculpture of the Queen in zinc, it was.

It is necessary to trace a little more fully the pedigree of what Cole called 'an intellectual festival of peaceful industry' on a scale without precedent. The Royal Society for the Encouragement of Arts, Manufactures and Commerce was itself an eighteenth-century foundation. Created in 1754 and committed to the benevolent proposition that 'Elegance and Ingenuity are most valuable when they contribute to the purposes of Virtue', it had held its first industrial exhibition in 1761, before Watt's invention of the steam engine and the great burst of late eighteenth-century industrial expansion which posterity was to treat as a revolution as portentous as that in France. The early language was that of the Enlightenment. The Exhibition, however, was a nineteenth-century idea, and its language, which was tinged with romanticism, took full account of the huge economic and social transformations from the invention of the steam engine onwards. Thus, the catalogue of the Society's 1847 exhibition stated its purpose as follows:

It is a universal complaint among manufacturers that the taste for good Art does not exist in sufficient extent to reward them for the cost of producing superior works: that the people prefer the vulgar, the gaudy, the ugly even, to the beautiful and perfect. We are persuaded that if Artistic Manufactures are not appreciated, it is because they are not widely enough known. We believe that when works of high merit, of British origin, are brought forward they will be fully appreciated and thoroughly enjoyed. We believe that this Exhibition when thrown open gratuitously to all, will tend to improve the public taste.

Albert had put it more economically the year before. 'To wed mechanical skill with high art is a task worthy of the Society of Arts and directly in the path of its duty.'

There was a complication. The 'improvement' of public taste was not as clear-cut an objective as the improvement of public health. Cole's desire to work through the newly founded Schools of Design was a matter of ideology as well as of organisation. He had strong theories and feelings, not universally shared, about what constituted the best designs. Albert may not have been fully aware of such complications. Nor was Cole fully aware, however, of the social complications. The organisation of the Exhibition was taken out of the hands of the Society of Arts in January 1850 and put into the hands of a Royal Commission and thereafter the aristocracy – and the politicians – were kept out of the picture. The Commission had two joint secretaries – Scott Russell of the Society and Sir Stafford Northcote, a future leader of the Conservative party in the House of Commons – and it included four sometime Prime Ministers – Russell, Peel, Stanley (later Lord Derby) and Gladstone. Its Deputy President was the Whig leader, Lord Grenville, a royal favourite of the future, whom Albert (despite his attachment to Peel) called 'the only working man on the commission'. Cole observed in his Autobiography 'somewhat wistfully', as Kenneth Luckhurst has put it, how after the founding of the Royal Commission his relations with the Prince were 'of necessity altogether changed'.

One new figure was coming more and more into the picture, at first against Cole's wishes – the scientist, Dr Lyon Playfair, who was to remain closely attached to the Prince after the Exhibition was over. His biographer describes him in words many of which might have been applied to Albert himself or to Cole.

His life, though it was lived without ostentation and parade, was undoubtedly one of the fullest and most useful lives of his time. It was emphatically a life of work, and of work not for the accumulation of wealth or the achievement of fame, but for the acquiring of truth and for the service of his fellow men.

He had wide interests and had risen by merit. Different though he was from Cole, we are obviously dealing with a type when we consider him and Cole, an Albertian type. Yet merit by itself was not enough. A Prince was necessary also. Of the three words in the tribute to Playfair which do *not* apply to Albert – ostentation, parade and fame – Albert never liked the first, but he was keenly interested in military matters, even in parade, and he was fully aware of the attractions of princely fame. So, too, were his middle-class admirers. Cobden made many attacks on 'feudalism' and on the 'feudal' attitudes not only of the English aristocracy, but of large sections of the English middle classes. Yet he could remark of Albert's fame that 'he would rather have his name associated with the great Industrial Exhibition of 1851, than be the Eugene or Marlborough of history, celebrated only for their triumphs on the battlefield'. Significantly, Albert's brother, the Duke of Coburg, saw the whole Great Exhibition in terms of 'fame'. 'Prince Albert was in the fullest sense of the word the soul of everything.' And 'splendour and pomp' were as much a part of the great festival as industry. Indeed, in his view, the Exhibition, unlike later exhibitions, was 'preponderantly aristocratic'. 'The high nobility undertook the representation of England in a manner such as there has since been no occasion for.'

Albert was anxious that permanent advantages should accrue from the Great Exhibition, and he knew well enough that both the arts and sciences had to be cultivated lovingly and regularly whether or not there were great dramatic events associated with them. There had to be continuous involvement. His great new idea was that with an Exhibition surplus of £186,000 thirty to forty acres of land should be bought in Kensington Gore and four new national institutions should be created corresponding to the four great sectors of the Exhibition – raw materials, machinery, manufactures and plastic arts, as in the Exhibition itself 'of all nations'. But his idea had other implications. 'If I examine what are the means by which improvement and progress can be obtained in any branches of human knowledge', he wrote in one of the most fascinating of all his memoranda,

I find them to consist of four. First: personal study from books. Second: oral communication of knowledge by those who possess it to those who wish to acquire it. Third: acquisition of knowledge by ocular observation, comparison and demonstration. Fourth: exchange of ideas by personal discussion. Hence I would provide there in special reference to the wants of each of the four great sections (1) a library and rooms for study: (2) lecture rooms: (3) a convenient area covered by glass: (4) room for conversazione, discussions and industrial meetings. The surplus space might be laid out as gardens for public enjoyment and instruction and be so arranged as to admit of the future erection of public monuments to a well-arranged plan.

The facilities should be 'open to men of all nations', he said, and it was with this in mind that his secretary, Sir Charles Phipps, wrote to Playfair in September 1851, 'The longer the Prince considers and weighs the subject of the disposal of the surplus, the more convinced he becomes that no arrangement for its appropriation can be satisfactory that does not include provision for all the interests of the world.'

The object must not be so much the founding of institutions through which Great Britain may be raised to an equality, or maintain her stature over other nations, as the foundation of some establishment in which by the application of science and art to industrial proceeds, the industry of all nations may be raised in the scale of human employment: and where, by the constant inter-change of ideas, experience and its results, each nation may gain and contribute something. There is no doubt that in such an inter-change England would ultimately be the great gainer.

The Press received the Prince's plan very coldly, although it had useful support behind the scenes. Thus Disraeli, then the

Chancellor of the Exchequer, taking a completely different line from Gladstone, wrote to Albert in 1852 that it was his conviction that 'when realised the creation of your Royal Highness will form an epoch in the aesthetic and scientific education of the people of England'. And when the Kensington Gore land was purchased for £150,000 – the land consisted of 'fields intersected by narrow lines' – Lord Derby congratulated the Prince on having established an Institution 'perfectly unparallelled in its scope and design and calculated to confer lasting benefits of the highest character'. There was, indeed, in time to be a remarkable trans- formation of a whole area now near the centre of London, part of which, for example, was to be the site of a Natural History Museum on ground where partridges were still being shot in 1851. This was the site the critics called 'Albertopolis'. Yet Albert's idea of moving out the National Gallery to South Kensington was never realised.

The full scale of the Prince's plans was, and there was con- troversy all the way, indeed never realised. Albert dreamed not only of the creation of a new locality devoted to science and the arts but of 'centralising' there – he used the term – all the great national institutions concerned with the sciences and the arts except the oldest of these institutions, the Royal Society, which he believed had 'forfeited the sympathy of the generality of the public by its lethargic state and exclusive principles', and the British Museum, which he was content to see remaining in Bloomsbury if some of its collections were moved westwards. Yet relatively few societies moved there with the exception of the Royal College of Organists, the Royal College of Music, the Physical Society and the Royal Geographical Society. There was as much dislike of 'centralisation' in the arts and sciences as there was in public health. There was also Parliamentary oppo- sition to the Government continuing to keep the Royal Com- mission of 1850 in existence and in 1858, to the Prince's irritation, the link was snapped by Parliament.

What did survive was a Science and Art Department organising examinations, scholarships and prizes, and there was some initial integration, too, if not centralisation, as the proposal that Cole should be made Secretary of the Art Department, and Playfair the Secretary of the Science Department, was amended so that Cole became Inspector-General of both Departments and Playfair Secretary. The Department functioned not through the Board of Trade but through the Privy Council, and it provided a nucleus for institutionalised higher education not only in the metropolis but in the country. Institutions still located in South Kensington include the Royal College of Art, the Royal College of Music and Imperial College, the great specialised College of Science and Technology, incorporating the older Royal School of Mines, the Royal College of Science and the City and Guilds College. There are also located there many of the great national museums – the Victoria and Albert with a tiled portrait of Cole on one of its staircases, the Geological Museum, the Natural History Museum and the Science Museum. Appropriately the two great monuments to Albert – the Albert Hall and Gilbert Scott's Memorial, more of a shrine than a monument – are nearby, the latter in Hyde Park, itself the scene of the Exhibition. This remains an extraordinary complex, and as the historian C. R. Fay wrote in 1951, 'if we look with the eye of imagination, can we not see behind the Victorian buildings of South Kensington the shining glass structure of the original Palace standing in Hyde Park close by, the marvels it contained and the millions from all countries who came to visit and admire?'

The Great Exhibition of 1851 was a great metropolitan event, though it drew in large numbers of people from abroad and from the English provinces. The provinces had displayed an interest in exhibitions, intellectual as much as industrial, before the capital did, and both Cole and Playfair were familiar with their ways of life and aspirations. Increasingly during the 1850s they played a part in Albert's life. This was the golden age of English provincial culture and Albert's visits to great provincial cities, like Manchester, Leeds and Birmingham, were never chores: they provided him with information, interest and pleasure. He had already started his provincial trail in the 1840s with a memorable visit to Liverpool in 1846, the year of the repeal of the Corn Laws, when he opened the Albert Dock and proposed a toast 'Prosperity to British Commerce'. At the Mansion House banquet of 1850, 180 mayors of towns and cities were present, and it was Albert's task, above all else, to convince them that what he said mattered.

The only two provincial events of the 1850s which I have time to describe in any detail – and they both require detail if their mood is to be recaptured – were the laying of the foundation stone of the new Midland Institute in Birmingham in 1855, and the opening two years later of the Art Treasures Exhibition in Manchester, Birmingham's great rival provincial city. The Midland Institute, which was described in 1911 as 'the mother of educational activities', was concerned both with the arts and with science at a time when the only picture in the possession of the Town Council of Birmingham was the little-known local artist Edward Coleman's composition 'Dead Game', and when there was more craft than science in local industry, the industry of small workshops. The Institute, first mooted in the 1840s, had close connections with the School of Design, and one of its further objects, strongly supported by Charles Dickens, was the appreciation of literature. Yet great stress was placed too on penny science lectures and a 'museum of models' referred to by Dickens himself: 'it would be an institution', he said in 1852 three years before the Prince's visit, 'where industry might exhibit the various processes of manufacturing machinery and thereby come to new results'.

Dickens had not been so forthright or so optimistic in 1851 at the time of the Great Exhibition, only the year before. By 1855, however, on the occasion of Albert's visit, Hyde Park's Great Exhibition in a Crystal Palace, now moved out from Central

London to Sydenham, belonged very much to the past. In 1851 one of the main themes was international peace through art, science and free trade: in 1855 Britain was at war in the short-lasting but highly popular Crimean War against Russia, a war which was particularly popular in Birmingham, which manufactured weapons among almost everything else. It is refreshing that in such circumstances Albert's message was consonant with everything he had ever said or was to say. He was under attack at this time, but he remained consistent and forthright. 'I must heartily join with you', he said, 'in congratulating the country that not even such a war as that in which we are now engaged, calculated as it is to enlist our more immediate interest, can divert Englishmen from the noble work of fostering the arts of peace and endeavouring to give a wider scope to the blessings of freedom and civilization.'

The Manchester Art Treasures Exhibition of 1857 took place in somewhat more propitious political circumstances, but in a year of financial crisis which directly affected the cotton trade. Manchester was described by Nathaniel Hawthorne as 'the rudest great town in England', but it was a great concentration both of wealth and poverty, and its Royal Institution was seeking to realise both provincial and national objectives. Albert's faith in educating the public in the appreciation of art by showing a far wider range of art treasures than it had been possible to display in the Crystal Palace in 1851 was abundantly realised, and for once the venture was blessed by Ruskin too. Many of the treasures came from Albert's own collection: it included a picture of Manchester by William Wyld which he had commissioned.

After receiving a Mancunian delegation in 1856, Albert left much of the work of organising the exhibition to Gustav Waagen, who knew more about 'how much art' and of what kinds could be found in different places in England than any of his contemporaries. He had first visited England in 1838 and followed up his visit with his controversial book *Works of Art and Artists*

76

in England and fourteen years later his *Treasures of Art in Great Britain.* The guiding ideas were still Albert's, however, notably the central idea that the success of the Exhibition would be judged by 'the usefulness of the undertaking...in the educational direction'. It was not enough to gratify curiosity: it was necessary to 'elevate' the mind of the viewer. 'You have done well', Albert told his audience at the opening, 'not to aim at a mere accumulation of works of art and objects of general interest, but to give your exhibition by a scientific and historical arrangement an educational character – thus not losing the opportunity of teaching the mind as well as gratifying the senses. And manifold are the lessons which it will present to us.'

This is the right place to end, for if the God of the Victorians offered manifold blessings, it was the task of Victorian men, prophets and critics alike, to explain how manifold were the lessons and what they were. I have said little about music, which Albert composed, performed and appreciated, but it, too, was felt to carry with it a message or rather a set of messages, and Mendelssohn, who was greatly admired by Albert, was thought of as the contemporary composer who carried them best – through his life, more shortened even than Albert's, as much as through his music. In considering music, too, Albert and the Queen were in more close rapport than they were in considering science and the arts, particularly the former, for the Queen could, of course, paint and draw and had been interested in music (with her own clearly defined opinions) even before she and Albert met.

One anecdote about music provides a fitting ending to this lecture. On the occasion of the Christening of the Prince of Wales in 1842, attended by Friedrich Wilhelm IV of Prussia as sponsor, there was a full choral service, and Prince Albert's good taste was said to have been shown when, after a new anthem was offered to him for the conclusion of the service, he said, 'No. If the service ends with a new anthem, we shall all go out criticising the music. We will have something we all know – something in which we can all share.'

No lecture can end with any better sentiment. There are many new things to discover about Albert, though the documentation is often sadly lacking. But from the evidence already at our disposal we know that we are dealing with an outstanding person who was always anxious to get others to 'share'. He was best able to share his views with a small group of 'Albertian' people, but he looked beyond their ranks to the millions outside. He combined enjoyment in art with a persistence of moral endeavour so that it is appropriate that this lecture having begun with a sermon and a text, his own words should provide the necessary text in conclusion.

QUEEN VICTORIA AND PRINCE ALBERT IN COBURG

SIR ROBIN MACKWORTH-YOUNG

IT WAS a truly inspired initiative on the part of our hosts to combine a seminar on Prince Albert with a pilgrimage to the land of his birth. Delightful as the experience has been – and here I would like to add my contribution to the heartfelt thanks already expressed by my distinguished colleagues for the friendliness and generous hospitality we have met on all sides – our excitement is naturally as nothing beside that of Queen Victoria when her husband first brought her to his childhood home. Much as she longed to come, it was not until the summer of 1845, five and a half years after their marriage, that she was able to make the expedition.

Thanks to a vivid account in her diary, supported by an excellent series of watercolours from her personal collection, we can relive the experience with her. The thoughts which animated her mind at the time may have been a good deal less weighty than those more characteristic of her husband, of the kind which have provided the focus for this gathering; but the lighter side of life also has its place. If this seminar may be likened to a symphony, perhaps Queen Victoria may provide the scherzo.

For her the journey to Coburg was doubly exciting. Not only was this the one place where she felt she really belonged as the Prince's wife – 'If I was not what I am', she wrote, '*this* would

79

have been my real home'; but she had never been to Germany before; and with Germany as a whole she had powerful links through her lineage. In fact her ancestry was actually more than ninety-nine per cent German. Her mother was of course, like her husband, a Coburg, and her father was a member of the House of Hanover. To find her first non-German ancestor we must go back as far as the grandmother of King George I: Elizabeth, Queen of Bohemia, consort of the 'Winter King', and daughter of King James VI of Scotland and I of England. She was one of Queen Victoria's one hundred and twenty-eight great-great-great-great-great-grandparents. Another ancestor in that generation was French, and so far as I know all the remaining one hundred and twenty-six were German. With such a pedigree it is not surprising that Queen Victoria felt a natural affinity for the German language. Now for the first time she heard German spoken in the streets. 'To hear the *people* speak German', she wrote, 'and to see German soldiers etc. seemed to me so singular.'

Their goal was Coburg, but to reach it they must cross territory belonging to the King of Prussia. So their first stopping-place was Schloss Brühl, between Cologne and Bonn. This fairy-tale palace is still used today for the entertainment of visitors of state, and our present Queen savoured its delights during her visit to Germany two years ago. 'Its marble staircase', wrote Queen Victoria, 'is truly magnificent.'

From here a visit to Bonn, where Prince Albert had been a student at the university, was obligatory. They went over the small house in which he had lived, and they witnessed the unveiling of a statue to Beethoven. 'Unfortunately', wrote the Queen, 'when the statue was uncovered it turned its back.' Then, after a journey up the Rhine, broken by a stay at Stolzenfels, riverside seat of the King of Prussia, they set out for Coburg in their travelling chaise. On the afternoon of the following day they crossed the Main at Lichtenfels. 'I began to feel so moved', wrote the Queen,

1   Coburg and the Festung from Weckereut (William Callow)

2   Prince Albert's house during his time at Bonn University (C. Hohe)

3 Ketschendorff, the house used by King Léopold and Queen Louise during the visit of Queen Victoria and Prince Albert (H. Brückner)

4 Schloss Ehrenburg, the town residence of the Dukes of Coburg (W. Corden)

5   The Arcades at Coburg (H. Brückner)

6   Reception room, Schloss Ehrenburg, where Queen Victoria
and Prince Albert were welcomed (Rothbart)

7   Rosenau, birthplace of Prince Albert (Douglas Morison)

8   Bedroom at Rosenau used by Queen Victoria and Prince Albert
in 1845 (Rothbart)

so agitated on coming near the Coburg frontier. At length in about three quarters of an hour we saw flags, and people drawn up in lines – and in a few minutes more we were welcomed by *dear Ernest* in full uniform. We came to an *Ehrenpforte* where we were received by the *Landdirektor*, and then drove to Ketschendorff, the pretty little house of our dear late grandmother, where we found Uncle Leopold and Aunt Louise, who got into our carriage. We came to another Ehrenpforte where Herr Begner, the Bürgermeister (a singular looking old man with a most extraordinary large nose) addressed us, and was quite overcome. A number of young girls dressed in white with green wreaths and scarves, standing on either side, presented us with bouquets and verses. I cannot say *how* much affected I felt in entering this dear old place and with difficulty I resisted crying; the beautifully ornamented town, all with wreaths and flowers, the numbers of good and affectionate people, the many recollections connected with this place, *all* was so affecting.

We then proceeded slowly to the Palace, which is very handsome and the Platz in front of it, which is very fine and so open. There is a terrace with arches just built before the Hofgarten which is extremely handsome.

The band played as we came in, and numbers of young girls dressed like the others threw wreaths into the carriage. We drove under an archway up to the foot of the stairs, where we assembled all the family *en grande tenue*. Good Ernest led me upstairs into the fine Drawing Room where we all stayed talking, and drank chocolate. Mama, Aunt Julia (who *both* embraced me, and were much overcome, as I was also (& how could it be otherwise)) dear Alexandrine, Mama Marie,[1] the Grand Duke of Baden,[2] our cousin Linette Reuss – and on either side of the staircase were: dear Uncle

---

[1] Prince Albert's stepmother and also his first cousin.
[2] Alexandrine's father.

Mensdorff, Alexander Würtemberg, Ernst Würtemberg,[1] Fritz Baden,[2] Leopold, Charles, Hugo, Alphonse, Alexander & a young Prince Max of Fürstenberg[3] – the staircase was *full of cousins*. All the ladies and gentlemen were there. It was a very affecting and beautiful moment, which I shall *never* forget.

At $\frac{1}{2}$ past 6 we entered another carriage, a small open one, with Ernest, and drove up to the *dear Rosenau*.

The dear Rosenau is lovely, so peaceful, and the situation – a high one – so fine. The House is very peculiar. The ground on which it is built is uneven, for on our side the rooms are 2 stories high and on the other side are on the ground floor. You go up a winding staircase – a broad one – and immediately on the left are 3 rooms...my little dressing room, our dear little bedroom, the paper of which is painted to represent trellis-work – with flowers – and my sitting room – a very nice room with 4 windows...

All the family...came to dinner, including Linette Reuss who is a very amiable old maid whom Albert & Ernest are always and have always been teazing. The Hofchargen – M. de Löwenfels – Hofmarshall M. de Wangenheim – walked before us with sticks to dinner. Besides them some members of Ernest's household and a Prince Sale (a Javanese and great friend of Ernest's) dined with us. We dined in the Marmorsaal [The Marble Hall] – where dear Albert was christened – which is a beautiful room with columns and ornamented with gold. The table was in the shape of a horse-shoe, and everything very handsome, exceedingly well done and well served and *bien grand*. Much better served than at the King of Prussia's.

Wednesday August 20

How happy and how joyful we felt on wakening to feel ourselves *here*, at the *dear* Rosenau, my dearest Albert's

[1] Brothers of Mama Marie.   [2] Brother of Alexandrine.
[3] Cousin to Alexandrine.

birthplace, and favourite place! I told him I was *so delighted,* so *over happy,* so *over thankful,* to be able to come here at last, which we so wished, and which we so feared would never be the case. I felt as if I should like always to live here with my dearest Albert, and if I was not what I am – *this* would have been my real home. But I shall always consider it *my 2nd home,* and as *my 2nd country.* My dearest Albert was *so so* happy to be here with me – it is like a beautiful dream. At 8 o'clock the singers of the Theatre sang chorales, which touched me so; music, when one is much '*bewegt*' and moved, is so very affecting. The old clock plays an air out of the Freischütz – which always makes me inclined to cry.

Before breakfast we went upstairs (two flights) to where my dearest Albert & Ernest used to live, when they were in the Nursery and up to the last moment. It is quite in the roof – with a small bedroom on either side, in *one* of which they both used to sleep with their tutor Florschütz (whom they called the 'Rath'). The view is beautiful, and the paper is still full of holes from their fencing – and the very same table upon which they were dressed when little is there.

After breakfast we walked out with Ernest & Alexandrine to the Schweizerei [The Swiss Cottage], where they are now living and which is so charming. It is a real Swiss cottage with the cows and bulls below, and above some very pretty little rooms which you get to by a staircase outside. Dear Albert & I drove home.

At a little past 1 we set off for the Festung. Albert & Ernest & M. de Wangenheim, Anson & Wylde rode, Lord Liverpool & Lord Aberdeen following in another carriage. Alexandrine and the ladies going in a pretty little open carriage, with 4 horses. We drove by such a pretty road, across wooden bridges, up a winding road thro' woods. We stopped at the outside of the Festung while Uncle and Louise met us, and walked up.

The interior of the Court and the whole interior is most beautifully arranged & restored by poor dear Papa. The Fortress is extremely old, part of it about the 12th century. We went up the wooden staircase & looked down at the 2 bears who are always kept there, & fed them with paper!! & then we went into Luther's rooms where there are still parts of his bedstead and chair which are most precious relics. From here we entered the Armory, which contains many highly curious suits of armour, amongst them Duke Bernhard of Saxe-Weimar's – he was a famous Reformer.

There are several other beautiful rooms; one, on the ceiling of which there are upwards of 800 different rosettes!! The old & new carving is so well matched, that it is all in keeping. One of the most curious rooms is the Horn Room, in which John Casimir's hunting and shooting exploits are all represented in exquisite inlaid pictures.

We then went on the bastions, from which there is a glorious and *most* extensive view, and the effect of light was wonderful. Coburg below, with the Thüringer Wald, & all the fine mountains towards Gotha in the background. There is such a constant movement on the ground, it looked quite Italian.

Some watercolours reproduced here were actually painted about twenty years later by Theodore Rothbarth.* By then the railway had come to Coburg. Mr Appeltshauser has pointed out that the resplendent Schloss which you can see in one of them is actually the new railway station.

We walked down to the new Arkaden, & drove home. You pass through a little village called Dörfles. All the people looked so comfortable and happy: you see them working in the fields very hard, and very actively.

* Several of the views of Coburg illustrating this article are signed 'Rothbart' and 'T. Rothbarth'. It is clear from other works signed by these artists and from payments in the Royal Archives that several members of the Rothbart family were active as artists during the nineteenth century. Any definite identification of hands is not yet possible.

9 Sitting room at Rosenau (Rothbart)

10 The Marble Hall, Rosenau (Rothbart)

11   Room used by Prince Albert and Prince Ernest as
children, Rosenau (Rothbart)

12   The Swiss Cottage (H. Brückner)

13　The Festung, Coburg (T. Rothbarth)

14　The moat bridge to the Festung, Coburg (artist unknown)

15   Luther's room at the Festung (Rothbart)

16   The interior of the theatre, Coburg, with the audience standing to receive
Queen Victoria and Prince Albert (Rothbart)

Immediately after dinner we drove to the theatre where we assembled in a beautiful salon all the Family with their suites. Dear Uncle Ferdinand was also there, who I am happy to say I find *not* looking ill, though thinner – & has lost his hair very much. We then went into the Theatre, which is an extremely pretty one, painted with blue, white and gold. We were all seated in a very large box, in the middle of the house. The good people received us most kindly, & *all* sang God Save the Queen, adapted to German words. They then gave the 'Huguenotten' *en entier* & extremely well. Igatschek sang & acted *Raoul* magnificently. The scenery, decorations, addresses etc. were so well done. We came home at 1.

Thursday August 21

At 12 we got into a funny but comfortable carriage – the first seat like a charabanc where we sat, & behind a 4 seated carriage with seats opposite to one another at right angles to our seat, in which our 2 ladies, Lord Aberdeen and Lord Liverpool were seated, Ernest riding. We drove up to the Kalenberg, through Neusis. The ascent is gradual but steep. We got out before we got to the very top and walked to the Theeplatz in order to get a view of the castle. We then walked up into the Court up a flight of steps to a charming terrace with flowers. We then went up a winding staircase into their drawing room and Alexandrine's sitting room, both elegantly furnished & full of bronzes, china and pictures, and the view beautiful, particularly from one large window. It is a delightful spot, but *I prefer our dear Rosenau*. We went back, seated as we came, from the Rosenau. The pavement in Coburg is dreadful.

We came home a little before 4. I feel so *at home* here, as if I had *always* been here. At a little after 4 we dined. The evening was glorious – everything so green, so bright – the Festung looking so fine. And we talked & laughed so merrily with the dear Mensdorffs, Charles & Ernest – such a Familien-Verein is so delightful. Lord Aberdeen is pleased 'beyond every-thing' with *our dear* little country, & thinks it is so beautiful, & the people so good and comfortable.

At 6 we drove to Coburg to the Palace with Ernest and Alexandrine. I was dressed in my red Crêpe de Chine, with a wreath of natural flowers and my diamonds. We then went into the Vorzimmer where were assembled all the Ladies & Gentlemen & Ernest's very numerous and *umständig* Hofstaat, Löwenfels & M. de Wangenheim carrying a long wand, surmounted by a crest. We proceeded to where Mama lives – where were assembled all the Family and Herr-schaften, all very smart – all the gentlemen in uniform.

We then went into the Riesensaal, a very handsome large room supported by giants terminating in a pedestal. We all stood in a row – Ernest & Alexandrine to my right, who presented everybody, and Louise, and then Uncle when the gentlemen came, standing near me, & next to them dearest Albert – after which came the rest of the family – all the attendants standing behind us; Löwenfels & Wangenheim only stood in front. First of all came the Ladies, then the Diplomats, then Household [*Angestellten*], strangers, deputa-tion of Burghers, *Kaufleuten* and *Handwerkverein.* And they behaved so well, making such much better bows than *any* of *our* people at the levées. When they had gone by we *cercléd* with the ladies who had remained. Everything was so *ausständig* and well managed. We drove home to the dear Rosenau at ½ p. 10.

Friday August 22

At ½ p 1 we drove to the Palace at Coburg, where the whole family was assembled. We stepped out on the balcony which overlooks the Court and saw the procession of children from the different schools. It is called the Gregorius Fest. All the children walked 2 by 2 into the Court, headed by their schoolmaster and a Band. The boys 1st and then the girls, some in costume as shepherdesses etc. and a little boy as a powdered gentleman etc. and the greater part of the girls in white with green. There were 1300 I believe. Three girls came upstairs & presented us with a *Gedicht,* to the tune of God Save the Queen, which the children sang well. After this we drove to the Anger, a meadow quite close to the town. There were two tents pitched – decorated with flowers, & open at the sides, under which we were to dine, & all the children were in front of us. A band played the whole time. We walked round all the children and then sat down to dinner. The children began to dance, valses, polkas etc. & so merrily – & they played games and were so truly happy – & the evening was so beautiful the whole so animated – the good people so quiet. . .Some of the prettiest girls & the little powdered boy were brought round to us & got sugar plums. At 6 we drove back to the Schloss and I rested & dear Alexandrine who is so fond of me sat with me.

Then I dressed in a light blue Tarlatan with lace, the whole family & suites assembled, & we went into the Riesensaal, where all the company was assembled for the Ball, about 2 or 300. The ball began with a Polonaise. A couple go first always as Vortänzer – I danced with Ernest, all the Herrschaften joining & when I came back to my place I took one with Uncle Leopold, then a gallop with Fritz Baden (who is very amiable) and several more dances.

We then went to supper which was most handsomely served in a fine room. The Grand Duke observed that nothing could be better done than it is here; the Court is so dignified – the whole dinner & *cuisine* so good, the equipages & horses so fine, the Theatre – everything is *so well* done. Nothing was near so well done at Brühl, tho' on a grander scale.

We only came home at ½ past 2.

Saturday August 23

At ½ past 9 we breakfasted with Ernest & walked with him to the Bade Häuschen and Fischer Häuschen on the little river, which are so pretty, & drove home.

At 11 we drove with dear Alexandrine, whom we picked up at the Schweizerei (just now that dear old clock is playing while I write, so wehmüthig) & Lady Canning, Ernest driving from the box to the old Schloss Kirche which is a long fine Chapel, & from there to the 'Kabinet', which is dear Albert & Ernest's collection of stuffed birds – insects – minerals – all sorts of curious things & autographs – to which he is continually making additions & I have helped. We went from here to Feodore's rooms & paid her a visit, & sent for Bratwürste which is the national dish of Coburg – from the Markt & eat them & drank some of the excellent Coburg beer – they are so good [together].

From here we drove to Ernst Würtemberg's charming villa, which is in a lower range of hills – halfway between the Kalenberg & Coburg. Ernst did us the honours of his charming house which is so elegantly furnished & full of fine china etc. & ought to have a Hausfrau. We drove home at 4. It was much the warmest day we have had. A little before 5 we dined, and later drove to the theatre where we saw Schiller's tragedy of 'Die Braut von Messina' very fine & very well acted, but dreadfully tragic. We came home at ½p.11.

Sunday August 24

At ½p. 11 we drove to the St Moritz Kirche, a fine large church in fact the cathedral of the town. The bells ringing sounded so beautiful. The clergy received us at the door & Gensler addressed a few words to me, expressive of his great joy at receiving the great Christian Queen who was descended from the Saxon Dukes who were the first Reformers, and at the door of the church where the Reformation was first

17 Schloss Kalenberg, the summer residence of the
Dukes of Coburg (Lady Canning)

18 The hall of the giants, Schloss Ehrenburg (Rothbart)

19　Children's fête on the 'Anger', Coburg, witnessed by the
Queen and Prince Albert (H. J. Schneider)

20　The market place, Coburg (artist unknown)

21 The chapel in
Schloss Ehrenburg (Rothbart)

22 Moritzkirche, Coburg
(artist unknown)

23 Woodland scene with shooting stand and boars (T. Rothbarth)

24 Distant view of the Festung from Oeslau (Louis Gurlitt-Gelhaar)

25 The bedroom used by Queen Victoria and Prince Albert at
Schloss Ehrenburg (Max Brückner)

preached. The church was immensely full, & is a fine large church with a very curious & ancient altar piece, & the windows of that pointed architecture. The service is much like the Scotch only with more form, less prayer, & more singing. The singing of the more beautiful Chorales by the whole congregation was the most impressive *erbauend* thing imaginable. They sang 'wachet auf' – 'Wer nur den lieben gott lässt walten' etc. Gensler presented a fine sermon.

We drove home from here. All the peasants in their smart dresses looked so pretty, with such bright colours – & all so attentive. The men, when properly dressed, wear jackets with steel buttons – leather breeches & stockings, & a fur cap.

At 3 we drove out to Schönstädt, and on to Mönchröden. This put us all so much in mind of Scotland, the same fir wood – only spruce & silver fir instead of Scotch firs – & the same wild plants. We drove up to an enclosure. Here we got out & all went up into a highish stand, which had been charmingly arranged on purpose, & then the wild boars were let in – 30 in number, including very large ones, & quite young ones – & they ran about, & quite alarmed me; they are most ferocious looking animals. At length all were sent out again, except one 'ein übergelaufenes' which had no tusks, & this was speared – in a most dexterous manner, for it requires great courage & great skill. One of Ernest's Jägers, Wittig by name, went down into the enclosure & stood with his spear ready, upon which the animal ran, & made a most shocking noise. Then mortally wounded it ran away again, & again returned, was again speared & immediately killed. It must be a very dangerous sport; they are generally shot however. After this we walked away & then got into our carriage & drove home.

At luncheon we had such delicious *mehlbrei*. After dinner we sat & talked together & broke up at ½ past 10. I *can't think* of going away from here. I count the hours, & cried yesterday at the thought – for I have a *feeling* here which I *can't* describe, a feeling as if my *Childhood* also had been spent here.

Monday August 25

Again such a beautiful day. Really *the heavens bless and protect our visit* to this *dear country*. Dearest Albert & Ernest went into town where I fear they will be all day, & I have been writing ever since. I sat down with dear Alexandrine in our breakfast *Plätzchen* & sketched a lovely housemaid in her costume.

Tuesday August 26

To celebrate *this dear day in my beloved Husband's country & birthplace* is *more than I ever hoped for*, & for which I am *so* thankful! May God Almighty ever bless & protect this adored being to all eternity & that He will!

I wished him so warmly joy when the singers sang (like on the other morning) & then the band played a Chorale, a Reveil, & several other things beautifully, among others the March & O Isis & Osiris from the Zauberflöte. I was so touched by the music.

When dressed I arranged the table with good Ernest & Alexandrine in the largest blue drawing room. It was '*geschmückt*' with flowers & cakes for dear Albert. The day was the finest & warmest brightest summer's day, which is *de bon augure* for dearest Albert. I gave him a little picture by Thomas Uwins of Cupid & Psyche (which he always wished to have) a stick with a coral top & a little snuff box. From Mama he got trifles, and from Ernest a beautiful chessboard. We fetched dearest Albert and he was much pleased. We were soon joined by all the family. With them we breakfasted in our Plätzchen & it was the hottest summer's day you can imagine. The band played & it was so pretty. To think that this is the last day *here*, where I am so happy, breaks my heart.

Some of the peasants came up in gala dress – 2 by 2 – with music, many of the women with wreaths on their heads & the men's hats decorated with ribbons or flowers. The first couple came up to us & the woman presented a wreath to my dearest Albert & the man a nosegay to me – saying at the same time '*Ich gratuliere zum Geburtstag von Ihrem Gemahl, wünsche dass er recht lang leben möge und dass Sie bald wiederkommen sollen*'. They danced shouting (*jauchzend*) in that peculiar way they have here, which they do whenever they do not dance for pleasure. They waltzed, and danced the polka extremely well.

After this we walked down to Oeslau where there is an old castle or house. It was most intensely hot. We drove home with Ernest & Alexandrine, dropping them at the Swiss cottage. I rested, took some luncheon, sang with dear Albert, including his dear duet, & then we walked out. We walked down the steps below our breakfast *Plätzchen* where there is a beautiful rock with a small waterfall, with a very pure stream, & then along the valley which leads to the *Bade Häuschen*, where the people were making hay. We met Lord Aberdeen here, & while dear Albert was talking to him, I sat down & drew, & one or two of the women who were making hay came close to me and said, as all the country people do here 'Guten Abend' – whenever you meet them they say 'Guten Tag' or 'Guten Abend' & it is so well meant; & upon my replying something about the weather she began to talk. They are so friendly, so good natured & so simple. The *Verhältniss* between them & their superiors is so pleasant. She had her 2 little children there & I gave her some money & she shook my hand for it. I don't think she the least knew who I was.

From here we walked by the rock again, where dear Albert made me taste the excellent water, & then we walked to the opposite side to see the little Festung which Albert & Ernest dug & made when they were children & which has remained perfect. There are such charming walks about the dear Rosenau. We walked fast home at quarter to 5. I ran upstairs to see Anson's room, which is the *one where my dearest Albert was born this day 26 years ago*!

We dined at 5, with all the family. I sat between *the beloved birthday* & Uncle Leopold. The band played as they did last night. *It is 12 years ago* since my dear Albert spent his birthday at the Rosenau. His health was drunk with a '*Dusch*'. At 8 we went to the Marmorsaal where there were some of the ladies from Coburg where we had a concert. Igatschek the singer & M Drouet, who played beautifully on the flute, were the performers. Dear Albert's duet & one by Ernest were sung.

We got to bed before 11. *So sad* I was & dearest Albert also, that this was our last evening in the dearest, peaceful Rosenau! God will grant that we may come here again ere long! And I am so grateful to have been able to come to the Rosenau.

They did come back to Coburg, but not for fifteen years. By this time the railway had arrived, and they travelled all the way by train, using the King of Bavaria's carriage. Sadly for them, their reception was muted, because the court was in mourning for the Prince's stepmother. Even more sadly for us, Queen Victoria's account of their stay is itself muted because all that survives of it are two abbreviated transcripts, one in Martin's biography of the Prince, and the other made many years later by her youngest daughter Princess Beatrice.

This time they did not, for some reason, stay in the Rosenau but in the Ehrenburg palace.

Meanwhile the older generation had moved on, and a younger generation had grown up. The Queen's mother, and her Uncle

26   The Festung from the Rosenau (Queen Victoria)

27   The interior of the ducal mausoleum (T. Rothbarth)

28   The housemaid Susanna in
local costume, 25 August 1865
(Queen Victoria)

29   Prince William of Prussia,
at the age of two, later
Kaiser Wilhelm II (Queen Victoria)

30   Sketch of three haymakers (Queen Victoria)

31   'Market Day' (Queen Victoria)

32   View 'From my window',
in Schloss Ehrenburg (Queen Victoria)

33   'Moritzkirche'
(Queen Victoria)

34   'Woman with pannier'
(Queen Victoria)

35   'Seated old man' (Princess
Victoria, Crown Princess Friedrich)

36   The unveiling of the Prince Consort's statue in the Square,
Coburg, August 1865 (G. H. Thomas)

Léopold were now too old to come, and Aunt Louise was dead. Instead their eldest daughter Princess Victoria, known in the family as Vicky, who had been too young to accompany them in 1845 and was now married to the future Kaiser Friedrich III of Germany, was there to greet them, with her two-year-old son William (the future Kaiser Wilhelm II). 'Our darling grandchild, such a little dear...he was very good' wrote the Queen, an opinion which she was to modify in later years. But now 'dear little William' came to her sitting room every day before breakfast. 'Our grandchild' she wrote to her Uncle Léopold 'is a darling little clever child like father & mother.'

Once more they made a round of visits, the Festung, the Rosenau ('everything just as it was', she wrote, 'the pretty garden, lovely view etc.'), Kalenberg, the Schweizerei, Ketschendorf, Oeslau, the Bade Häuschen; and for the first time the Mausoleum or *Erbbegräbnis* 'erected' recorded the Queen 'by the whole family after Albert & Ernest's designs, in the Italian style. It is not at all gloomy.' Little did she think, when she wrote these words, that fifteen months later she would be planning a similar building for her beloved husband.

A few days later an event occurred which nearly brought that unthinkable catastrophe even closer. Prince Albert was being driven alone from Kalenberg to Coburg when his horses bolted and collided with the gates of the new level crossing. The Prince managed to avoid serious injury by jumping off the carriage just before the collision: but he was considerably bruised and cut, and had to keep to his room for the next day. Five days later, however, he was well enough to participate in a boar shoot. This time guns and rifles were used instead of the spear, and 'dear Albert shot 3'.

Other diversions included long discussions with the aged and trusted Stockmar, and sketching.

Just before leaving Coburg, the Queen wrote to her Uncle Léopold in Belgium: 'I trust we shall be able to come here often and make (what I am sure you will agree in) this dear place a sort of rendezvous & *point de réunion* for the family – with our children.'

Notwithstanding her tragic bereavement at the end of the following year the Queen tried to carry out this intention, making several more visits to Coburg, the first less than a year after the Prince's death. But now everything they had enjoyed together was tinged with sadness. Only on the Prince's birthday, 26 August, must there be no sign of mourning. That day was chosen in 1865 for the unveiling of the Prince's statue in the Markt. The Queen went in procession to the ceremony, and the horses and postillions of her four carriages wore the scarlet and gold Ascot livery 'for the first time' she wrote 'since my terrible misfortune – I was anxious for *this* day to do all possible honour to my beloved's memory. The guns were fired from the fortress', she went on,

> and the bells rung, in the peculiar German way, so different from ours. The scene was beautiful on the fine old market place, with its high-roofed houses, all decorated, every window crowded, the tribune full of people, the white clad maidens of the town, one half with the British, the other with the Saxon colours, standing on either side. The Ober Bürger-meister read an Address, the signal was given, and in one second the drapery fell away from the statue, which stood there, in all its beauty, so sad and grand. Another salute was fired, and again beating of drums and ringing of bells. An indescribable moment, which can never be forgotten.

So in that deeply personal account Queen Victoria relates how this ancient city honoured one of the greatest of its sons. And today, in partnership with the University of Bayreuth, it is honouring him again, and in a way that he would have appreciated even more keenly. Your guests, Mr President, are proud and privileged to have taken part.

PRINZ ALBERT UND EUROPA

KURT KLUXEN

DIE EPOCHE von der Julirevolution 1830 bis zum Regierungsantritt Bismarcks 1862 stand im Zeichen eines politischen Liberalismus, dessen Durchsetzung in Europa sich mit einem Namen verknüpft, der als nationales Gütezeichen galt und der britischen Politik einen persönlichen Stempel aufdrückte: Lord Palmerston (1784–1865), seit 1830 über viele Jahre immer wieder Außensekretär und schließlich britischer Premierminister (1855–8; 1859–65), genannt 'Old Palmy' und 'the most English Minister',[1] dessen zweites Kabinett mit Gladstone als Schatzkanzler und Lord John Russell als Außenminister das erste war, das sich mit Fug und Recht als 'liberales Kabinett' bezeichnen durfte. Als Palmerston am 18. Oktober 1865 die Augen schloß, war die britische Weltstellung durch den Sieg der amerikanischen Nordstaaten im Sezessionskrieg (1862–5), die neue europäische Politik Bismarcks und das Ende der französisch-englischen Entente von 1831 rückläufig geworden.

Palmerston betrachtete die Schaffung des Königreichs Belgien 1831 als sein größtes Werk für den europäischen Frieden. Vor seinem Ableben ließ er sich die wichtigsten Artikel des Belgischen Vertrags vorlesen, den er in London am 15. November 1831 mit Talleyrand als französischen Gesandten sowie mit Heinrich von Bülow für Preußen, Esterhazy für Österreich und Lieven für Rußland ausgehandelt hatte, wenn er auch erst mit der Einwilligung von Holland am 19. April 1839 zum anerkannten Bestandteil

[1] Donald Southgate, *The Most English Minister. The Policies and Politics of Palmerston*, London 1966.

111

der europäischen Friedensordnung wurde. Die Unabhängigkeit und immerwährende Neutralität Belgiens war die Frucht einer europäischen Einigung. Damit war ein Staat als Friedens- und Freiheitszone anerkannt, der sein Dasein einer nationalen Revolution verdankte und außerdem dem militärischen Zusammenwirken der beiden Westmächte in jener 'Entente cordiale', die der alte Talleyrand mit Palmerston zustande gebracht hatte. Palmerstons Verdienst war nicht zu überschätzen, da er als einziger Minister und Chairman der Londoner Konferenz der französischen und belgischen Revolution zu diesem Erfolg verhalf. Dieser 'Musterstaat konstitutioneller Freiheit' war künftig das Herzstück des westlichen Liberalismus, ein Staat, der aufgrund seiner Entstehungsgeschichte das Völkerrecht, also das 'ius publicum europaeum' zu einer nationalen Wissenschaft erhob.

Hier im Westen war eine nationale Revolution auf die Ebene einer europäischen Verfassung gehoben worden, ausgerechnet als im Osten die Nationale Revolution der Polen zur Sicherung ihrer konstitutionellen Rechte von 1815 scheiterte. Der Untergang Polens und die Geburt Belgiens waren spektakuläre Ereignisse, die die Spaltung Europas in einen freien Westteil und einen reaktionären Ostteil offensichtlich machten. Scheidelinie zwischen beiden waren die Elbe und der Böhmer Wald. Die Entente England-Frankreich setzte das Siegel unter die West-Ost-Halbierung, wonach im Westen neue liberale Verfassungs- und Rechtsprinzipien an Boden gewannen, während im Osten das Monarchische Prinzip, der Legitimismus und die Heilige Allianz ihren Vorrang behaupteten. Die Vereinbarkeit beider Prinzipien war für die erstrebte deutsche Einheit eine Lebensfrage. Sie war im Grunde das eigentliche Problem des 'Coburger Kreises' und der Coburger Politik. Und eben Palmerston war es, der diese Dynastie ins Spiel brachte – und zwar mit einem überraschenden Coup zur Sicherung des jungen belgischen Staates gegen russische und französische Interventionen. Er lancierte die Wahl Léopolds von Sachsen-Coburg zum 'König der Belgier' (21. Juli 1831) und dessen Heirat mit einer Tochter des Bürgerkönigs Louis Philippe, Louise von Orléans. Der 'coburgische Ulysses' (Treitschke) war nämlich die vermittelnde Figur zwischen den Machtinteressen, der den belgischen Staat 'vor sicherm Verderben'[1] rettete. Léopold (1790–1865) war nämlich Fürstensohn ohne Hausmacht, unter Zar Alexander russischer General gegen Napoleon, einstiger Gemahl der im Kindbett gestorbenen englischen Thronerbin Charlotte, zeitweilig griechischer Thronkandidat, überzeugter Whig-Anhänger und Freimaurer und präsumptiver Schwiegersohn des 'Königs der Franzosen', also in alle denkbaren Konstellationen verknüpft.

Mit ihm beginnt eine Familiengeschichte, die doch mehr ist als eine Fußnote der europäischen Geschichte. 'Onkel Léopold' gab den Auftakt zu jener Invasion der Coburger auf die Königsthrone, die das kleine Coburg ins Konzert der Großmächte hineinzog. Die machtpolitische Bedeutungslosigkeit des ernestinischen Kleinstaates stand im grellen Gegensatz zu den weitgespannten europäischen Beziehungen, welche die Familie sich planmäßig zu schaffen wußte. Damit trat ein neuer Menschenschlag in die Reihen des europäischen Hochadels, dem es ursprünglich vor allem auf die Unterbringung der zahlreichen Familienmitglieder ankam. Sie hatten keine Truppen hinter sich und bevorzugten Tinte, Feder und Papier oder auch – wie Treitschke boshaft bemerkte – den Kurszettel. Jedenfalls nahmen sie große Gedanken auf, die sich gewissermaßen beiläufig aus den Zeitereignissen ergaben und ihnen mancherlei Chancen boten. Die Coburger taten sich viel darauf zugute, daß ihr klug rechnender Weltsinn der konstitutionellen Freiheit am besten diene und ihr Haus dabei eine historische Aufgabe erfülle, die ihm offensichtlich von der Vorsehung gestellt sei. Sie alle hielten die Verbindung des monarchischen Prinzips mit dem liberal-konstitutionellen Gedankengut für den einzigen Ausweg zur Rettung des europäischen Friedens und ihrer eigenen Existenz.

[1] Heinrich von Treitschke, *Deutsche Geschichte*, Bd. IV, Leipzig 1889, S. 83.

Indessen gab es unter ihnen nur zwei wirkliche politische Talente, nämlich 'Onkel Léopold', den König der Belgier, und Prinz Albert, den zweiten Sohn des regierenden Herzogs Ernst I. und Gemahl der Königin Victoria von England. Dazu trat als Mentor und Berater des Hauses Christian Friedrich Freiherr von Stockmar (1787–1863), ein ehemaliger Coburger Arzt, der bereits auf den Londoner Konferenzen 1830–1 die Verhandlungen mit den Belgiern für Léopold geführt hatte. Er verkörperte den Typus des liberal-konservativen Politikers der Epoche, nämlich

einen Politiker, der das Staatsleben des modernen Europa als einen bildsamen, durch politische Intelligenz und aufgeklärten Liberalismus zu formenden Stoff ansah. Er diente der Monarchie, aber so, wie sie eben die Coburger repräsentierten: also weniger der alten, historisch festverwurzelten, als einer modernen, gewandt errungenen, die in geschickte Balance mit den übrigen modernen Staatskräften zu bringen war.[1]

Seiner Kühnheit und seinem Gedankenreichtum war der Aufstieg der Familie aus ihrer Bedeutungslosigkeit zu europäischer Geltung zu verdanken, wenn er selbst auch seine Kräfte allzu sehr 'für die Geschäfte des internationalen Heiratsbureaus'[2] der Coburger verschwenden mußte.

Albert aber und seiner Tätigkeit als Prinzgemahl und ständiger Berater der englischen Königin war zu verdanken, daß diese coburgische Politik das Gewicht einer europäischen Alternative gewann. Solange er lebte, blieb diese politische Alternative im Spiel, die ganz Europa auf liberal-konstitutionellen Fuß setzen wollte. Sein früher Tod am 14. Dezember 1861 war für den westeuropäischen Liberalismus ein empfindlicher Verlust, aber für den deutschen politischen Liberalismus eine Katastrophe. Mit Albert ging diesem die Stütze verloren, die ihn vor nationaler Verengung bewahrt und seine Weltläufigkeit und Integrationskraft gesichert hätte.

Im Grunde war der zwanzigjährige Prinz Albert von Sachsen-Coburg-Gotha, als er am 10. Februar 1840 seine Cousine Victoria

[1] Friedrich Meinecke, *Weltbürgertum und Nationalstaat* (hg. H. Herzfeld), München 1962, S. 314.   [2] Treitschke a.a.O., IV, 86.

von England heiratete, ein 'Nobody' für die Engländer, die ihre eigenen Erfahrungen mit Ausländern auf ihrem Thron hinter sich hatten und keinen Anlaß fanden, ihn besonders herzlich willkommen zu heißen. Er war nur der *zweite* Sohn Herzog Ernst I., der am 26. August 1819 in Rosenau bei Coburg zur Welt kam, also fast gleichaltrig mit der Königin war. Außerdem waren die Brüder Ernst und Albert seelisch belastet durch die Auflösung der elterlichen Ehe 1824 und den Tod der Mutter Luise von Gotha 1831 in Paris, sowie auch durch die lockere Lebensweise ihres Vaters.

Aber Baron v. Stockmar und 'Onkel Léopold' in Brüssel nahmen beide Prinzen in ihre Schule. Auch der Lehrer Alberts, Christoph Florschütz aus Coburg, war ein Liberaler und ermutigte seine Schüler sogar, Philosophie zu studieren. Die Reisen der Brüder nach Belgien, Italien und England, ihr Jura-Studium in Bonn 1837–8, wo sie Moritz August von Bethmann Hollweg, Vertreter der Historischen Rechtsschule und später preußischer Minister der 'Neuen Aera', sowie die Shakespeare-Vorlesungen des alten August Wilhelm Schlegel hörten, trugen dazu bei, daß Albert bei seiner Heirat den engen Verhältnissen seiner Heimat entwachsen war und seinen frühen Lebensernst mit Weltläufigkeit zu verbinden wußte.

Schon 1841 und endgültig 1842 errang Albert eine Vertrauensstellung als politischer Berater der Königin. Unter seinem Einfluß hielt sich die Krone von einer einseitigen Bindung an eine Partei frei und entwickelte mit der Zeit Regeln einer wechselseitigen Information. Indessen blieb es lange umstritten, inwieweit die Krone auf die Regierungspolitik Einfluß nehmen durfte oder gar an politischen Entscheidungen zu beteiligen war. Im langen Konflikt mit Palmerston (1848–51) ging es um die Grenzen der jeweiligen Machtbefugnisse und nicht nur um die wechselseitige Sicherung des Informationsstandes. Victoria und Albert kamen gar nicht auf den Gedanken, daß dabei Loyalitätskonflikte möglich waren, weil sie als praktische Legitimisten ihr Regierungsrecht als naturgegeben ansahen und die 'Bruderschaft der

Fürsten' sowie die Priorität der bestehenden Throne für unantast-
bar und selbstverständlich ansahen.[1]

Indessen strapazierte Albert die konstitutionelle Autorität
manchmal bis an ihre Grenze, ohne sich dessen voll bewußt zu
sein.[2] Er wandte sich sogar gegen Palmerstons Privatkorre-
spondenz mit Kaiser Napoleon III. als 'a novel and unconstitutional practice'.[3] Er selbst unterhielt indessen ungeniert ein
eigenes Informationsnetz mittels der verwandten oder befreun-
deten Fürstenhöfe, das ihm vielfach sogar einen Informations-
vorsprung verschaffte. Die wütende Pressecampagne gegen Albert
im Jahre 1854 nahm diese 'Coburger Verschwörung' aufs Korn,
womit offenbar der intensive Nachrichtendienst der Coburger
angesprochen war, der neben der amtlichen Politik einherlief.
Späterhin verlief die Zusammenarbeit zwischen Albert und
Palmerston reibungslos.[4] Dazu kam, daß die königliche Familie
als Musterbeispiel vorbildlicher Lebenshaltung galt. Alberts
Vorstellung von fürstlicher Verantwortung der Regierungspolitik
gegenüber war sein eigener Beitrag zur Theorie und Praxis der
Verfassungsmonarchie. Er wird jedoch erst verständlich, wenn
jenes dynastische Instrumentarium mitgesehen wird, das eine
eigenständige politische Mit- und Zuarbeit möglich machte. Wie
sah dieses anachronistische Instrumentarium aus?

Die Mutter des regierenden Herzogs Ernst I. (1806–44) legte
den Grund dazu. Sie schickte auf einen Wink der Zarin Katharina
der Großen ihre drei lieblichen Töchter nach Petersburg, wo
Großfürst Konstantin, der Bruder des Zaren Alexander I. sich für
die jüngste, Julie, entschied.[5] Diese friedlose Verbindung mit
Julie, die jetzt Großfürstin Anna Feodorowna oder im Familienkreis 'Tante Anna' hieß, bahnte Bruder Léopold den Weg auf den
belgischen Thron und ihre Fürsprache beim Zaren 1807 rettete
den Coburger Kleinstaat vor französischer Besetzung.

---

[1] vgl. Frank Eyck, *Prinzgemahl Albert von England*, Erlenbach-Zürich und Stuttgart
1961, S. 256.
[2] vgl. Roger Fulford, *The Prince Consort*, 1949; W. L. Burn, *The Age of Equipoise*, 1964.
[3] Southgate a.a.O., S. 360; Eyck a.a.O., S. 285.
[4] Southgate, a.a.O.   [5] Treitschke a.a.O., iv, 85.

Eine andere Schwester, Maria Luise Victoria, verwitwete Fürstin von Leiningen, heiratete 1818 den Herzog von Kent, den vierten Sohn König Georgs III., der bereits 1820 starb. Aus dieser Ehe ging eine Tochter hervor: Alexandrine Victoria (1819–1901; seit 1837 Königin von England). Die dritte Schwester, Herzogin Sophie von Coburg (1778–1835) heiratete den österreichischen General Emanuel von Mensdorff-Pouilly. Der Sohn Alexander von Mensdorff-Pouilly, von den Coburgern 'Vetter Mensdorff' genannt, wurde österreichischer Außenminister (seit 1864) und war als Ehemann der letzten Fürstin von Nikolsburg auch Fürst von Nikolsburg, der vergeblich mit seinen Privatdepeschen König Wilhelm I. von Preußen und Bismarck zu trennen versuchte, aber doch bald darauf als Schloßherr von Nikolsburg 1866 die Versöhnungsstrategie der Coburger, diesmal im Bunde mit Bismarck und dem preußischen Kronprinzen im preußisch-österreichischen Waffenstillstand zu einem guten Ende führte.

Ferdinand, der Bruder Herzog Ernsts I., war österreichischer General und heiratete die ungarische Gräfin Antoinette Kohary im Jahre 1816, die von Kaiser Franz auf Bitten von Herzog Ernst zur Fürstin erhoben wurde, wobei die Kohary-Güter als coburgisches Fideikommiß und selbständiges ungarisches Fürstentum anerkannt wurden.

Der jüngste Bruder von Ernst I. war jener Léopold, der zuerst die Tochter König Georgs IV. und englische Thronfolgerin Charlotte heiratete, die jedoch schon 1817 im Kindbett starb. Léopold blieb in England und wurde von dort auf den Thron als König der Belgier erhoben (1831–65). Dies gab den Anstoß für eine eindeutige Westorientierung der Coburger, die mit der Heirat des Prinzen Albert mit Victoria am 10. Februar 1840 endgültig war. Ein Sohn von Ferdinand von Coburg-Kohary heiratete Maria da Gloria von Portugal und wurde König von Portugal. Aus einem anderen Zweig Ferdinands gingen später die Könige oder Zaren von Bulgarien hervor.

Die Westorientierung kam auch darin zum Ausdruck, daß drei Kinder von König Louis Philippe, nämlich Louise, Clémentine und der Herzog von Nemours (mit einer Tochter Ferdinands), in die coburgische Familie einheirateten, so daß das quasilegitime Bürgerkönigtum von Orléans als gleichberechtigt galt. Der letzte große Coup dieser Heiratspolitik war die eheliche Verbindung des preußischen Kronprinzen Friedrich Wilhelm mit der Royal Princess Victoria, genannt Vicky, im Jahre 1858, eine Heirat, die von vornherein auf die liberale Konstituierung Preußens zielte.

Das Unzeitgemäße an diesen dynastischen Allianzen lag darin, daß sie weder durch religiöse noch nationale Gefühle beunruhigt waren. Bei den Coburgern fanden sich alle großen Denominationen Europas zusammen, wobei Léopold als evangelischer Fürstensohn, russisch-orthodoxer General, anglikanischer Prinzgemahl, griechisch-orthodoxer Thronkandidat und römisch-katholischer König, als Freimaurer und Vertrauensmann von Papst und Klerus alle Möglichkeiten in seiner Person vereinigte. Die Coburger befleißigten sich einer ökumenischen 'media via' in religiöser und nationaler Beziehung. Indessen blieb der Hausberater Baron von Stockmar stets deutscher Patriot ebenso wie Prinz Albert, der unentwegt an einer deutschen Reichsgründung interessiert war. Über den Familienkreis hinaus gab es eine liberale Gesinnungsgemeinschaft, den 'Coburger Kreis', zu welchem noch Waldeck, Altenburg, Leiningen, Nassau, aber auch Großherzog Karl Alexander von Weimar, Großherzog Friedrich von Baden, der Erbprinz Friedrich von Augustenburg, Prinz Wilhelm von Preußen, dessen Gattin Auguste von Weimar, dann Wilhelms Schwester Alexandrine, Großherzogin von Mecklenburg-Schwerin, der preußische Gesandte von Bunsen und viele bedeutende Persönlichkeiten aus der Umgebung der Höfe gehörten.

Die lebenslange Korrespondenz der Königin Victoria mit 'Onkel Léopold' oder auch die überaus intensive und eindrucksvolle Korrespondenz von Prinz Albert mit König Friedrich Wilhelm IV. und dessen Bruder Prinz Wilhelm von Preußen war

stets politischer Natur und auch als unmittelbare politische Ein-
flußnahme gedacht. Das waren zwar keine eigentlichen diplomati-
schen Noten, aber auch nicht unverbindliche Wünsche und
Meinungsäußerungen sondern ernstgemeinte Projekte, Memor-
anden, Konzeptionen und Vorschläge. Sogar Mahnungen und
Warnungen von einer erstaunlichen Aufrichtigkeit jenseits aller
Diplomatie fanden sich häufig, wobei dieser Kommunikations-
zusammenhang an sich schon sein eigenes politisches Gewicht
hatte. Daran waren auch die Frauen mit Victoria an der Spitze
beteiligt; nicht zu vergessen auch zahlreiche Vertrauensleute,
Zwischenträger, Agenten und geheime Personen. Dieses unkon-
stitutionelle, um nicht zu sagen verfassungswidrige Netzwerk war
nicht gerade eine politische Notwendigkeit, aber doch im ganzen
gesehen ein Segen, weil hier von Mensch zu Mensch zur Geltung
kam, was sonst im zwischenstaatlichen Verkehr verloren geht,
zumal ein deutliches Niveau an Honorigkeit und Aufrichtigkeit
selbstverständlich war.

Seit dem Jahre 1846 warb Prinz Albert für eine Politik der
europäischen Solidarität. Den Anstoß dazu gab die Annexion der
unabhängigen polnischen Republik Krakau durch Österreich im
November 1846. Dies geschah im Einverständnis mit Rußland
und Preußen, aber ohne Genehmigung der westlichen Signatar-
mächte von 1815. Sogleich am 11. und 21. Dezember 1846 schrieb
Albert besorgte Briefe an König Friedrich Wilhelm IV.,[1] die von
seiner Denkweise, seiner politischen Programmatik und seinen
prognostischen Fähigkeiten eindrucksvolles Zeugnis ablegen. Im
ersten Brief heißt es: 'Durch den unglücklichen Schritt Österreichs...ist...die Basis der Verträge erschüttert worden, auf
welcher das ganze Friedensgebäude und europäische Gleichgewicht...ruht.' Im zweiten Brief forderte er sogar den König auf,
die Heilige Allianz zu verlassen. Er verwies warnend auf 'das
Bewußtsein aller Völker Europas'.

[1] Archiv Windsor, H, 49.5; H, 49.21.

119

Daher muß ich befürchten, daß einem Kampf – zur Verteidigung jener Politik
geführt, welch Krakau vernichtete – die kräftigste aller Stützen, der 'Glaube der
Völker an die gerechte Sache' fehlen werde; denn in einem solchen Falle
werden...die Völker...sich bewußt sein oder werden, daß sie für politische
Maximen kämpfen sollen, die mit der Errungenschaft der heutigen europäischen
Zivilisation im grellsten und vernichtendsten Widerspruch stehen, und die
Völker werden...ihr Herz versagen und...der zwingenden Kraft des großen
moralischen Gesetzes, das diese Welt regiert, mehr gehorchen als ihren Regierungen. Und dann, gnädigster König, würde der Augenblick gekommen sein, in
welchem die deutschen Mächte zu spät bereuen werden, daß sie, in Vergessenheit
der größten aller Güter, auf den Segen des Rechts verzichtet und sich allein auf
die rohe Macht gestützt haben.

Albert warnte eindringlich, daß die flagrante Verletzung einer
einzigen Klausel der Wiener Verträge von 1815 das Gesamtwerk
in Frage stelle. Dann würde sogar der Rechtsanspruch Preußens
auf die Rheinlande nur noch ein de facto Anspruch sein. Albert
war offenbar durch die gleichzeitigen Erbfolge- und Heirats-
dispute in Lissabon, Madrid und auch Schleswig-Holstein 1846–7
aufs äußerste beunruhigt und zog sich hier auf einen Legitimismus
zurück, dem die Priorität der Throne maßgebend war.

Wenige Monate später kündigte der Sonderbundskrieg in der
Schweiz 1847 den Bankrott des Systems Metternich an, der sich
in den lombardischen Revolten gegen Österreich im Januar 1848
fortsetzte und in die Februarrevolution in Paris sowie in die
Märzereignisse von Berlin und Wien einmündeten. Victoria und
Albert standen in Bezug auf Italien zu Österreich und schämten
sich der Politik Palmerstons, der die italienischen Rebellen und
König Karl Albert von Sardinien unterstützte, der in ihren Augen
Verrat an der Bruderschaft der Fürsten geübt hatte. Sie waren
gegen General Cavaignac zur Rechten und gegen die französische
Republik zur Linken und auch gegen eine italienische Unabhängig-
keit. Palmerston betrieb dagegen eine kaum verhüllte Ein-
mischungspolitik, die ihn als 'Troublemaker' und als 'Apostel der
Revolution'[1] oder – nach den Worten von Fürst Schwarzenberg –
als 'öffentlichen Feind der europäischen Ordnung' erscheinen ließ.

[1] Southgate a.a.O., S. 191, 250.

Eine solche Politik widerstrebte dem Herrscherpaar. Beide wollten eine Politik 'beyond reproach' und beriefen sich auf 'the confidence of Europe' oder auch auf eine ideale öffentliche Meinung, die mehr von den Gentlemen am Hofe als von den Gazetten repräsentiert wurde. Für sie beide war moralische Integrität eine Bedingung integrer Politik. Die innere Ausgeglichenheit und Honorigkeit war ihnen Vorbedingung für ausgewogenes Handeln zur Wahrung der europäischen Balance und Contenance. Im Einvernehmen mit den Fürsten und in der Übereinstimmung mit den wahren Wünschen des Volkes sahen sie den besten Weg zur Lösung der deutschen und der europäischen Frage, ein Weg, wie er ja dann auch 1870 von Bismarck schließlich beschritten worden ist, nachdem er 1866 freilich eine widerrechtliche Annexionspolitik gegen Hannover, Schleswig-Holstein und Hessen sich geleistet hatte.

Der 'viktorianische Moralismus' der beiden war nur zum Teil Reaktion auf die lockeren Sitten am Hofe Georgs IV. oder auch Ernsts II. Er setzte öffentliche Verantwortlichkeit und individuelle Gewissensbindung des Herrschers in eins. Dies ging so weit, daß Albert zeitweilig das Niveau der Politik Palmerstons wegen seiner Privataffären für gefährdet hielt.[1]

In Wirklichkeit entsprang dieser Moralismus einer optimistischen Weltvorstellung, die der liberale Bürgersinn sich für seine Daseinsbedürfnisse zurechtgeschnitten hatte. Sie war geradezu das Schwungrad eines Liberalismus, der dabei war, sich der Welt zu bemächtigen. Das Zeitalter, 'the Age of Improvement', war vom Glauben an die Möglichkeit einer Weltverbesserung durchdrungen. Auch die Projekte der Coburger nahmen daran teil. Was daher kam, war aber alles andere als Schönfärberei und Flickschusterei, nämlich von Modernität und Kühnheit geprägte, wirklich zeitgemäße Zielsetzungen, wie Albert sie ja selbst in England mit Weltausstellung und Sozialpolitik zum Erstaunen der Zeitgenossen inauguriert hatte.

[1] Eyck a.a.O., S. 166.

Das Revolutionsjahr 1848 war für Albert ein Wendepunkt, insofern seine Stellung zwischen England und Deutschland ihm erlaubte, auf die deutsche Einheitsbewegung Einfluß zu nehmen. Er war selbstverständlich für die Ablösung des Metternichschen Systems. Sie sollte sich aber unter Wahrung der Rechte der Fürsten und ohne Störung des europäischen Gleichgewichts vollziehen. Er begeisterte sich für die deutsche Einheit, aber er hielt sie nur über eine Konstitutionalisierung für erreichbar. Der Sinn seiner umfangreichen Korrespondenz mit König Friedrich Wilhelm IV. war nur, ihn für den Verfassungsgedanken zu erwärmen, da nur auf dieser Basis eine Einigung Aussicht auf Erfolg haben konnte. Er dachte sogar an eine Rolle Deutschlands im europäischen Bezugsrahmen.

Wohl durch Alberts Einfluß kam in Preußen das Februarpatent 1847 zustande, das erstmals einen Vereinigten Landtag als Ansatz einer Gesamtverfassung zu gewähren schien. Dann drängte Albert die deutschen Fürsten schon im März 1848 zur Initiative. Auf seinen Rat ließ sich Prinz Wilhelm sogar in einem Wahlkreis in Posen als Kandidat für die Nationalversammlung in Berlin aufstellen. Er drängte andere Prinzen und Fürsten, in die Paulskirche zu gehen, darunter über König Léopold als Mittelsmann auch die österreichischen Erzherzöge.[1]

Schon Ende März 1848 legte Albert seinen ersten Verfassungsentwurf vor.[2] Danach sollten Kronen und Dynastien bestehen bleiben und einen Bundesstaat bilden. Ein Reichstag sollte aus indirekten Wahlen der einzelnen Länder hervorgehen, dem die Reichsminister begrenzt verantwortlich waren. Der Fürstentag als Oberhaus behielt ein Vetorecht und wählte den Kaiser. Der Wahlkaiser als 'Treuhänder der Gesamtheit' sollte den Fürsten die Furcht nehmen, ins Abseits geschoben zu werden. Die Solidarität und Bereitwilligkeit der regierenden Fürsten waren für seine Konzeption unabdingbar.

[1] Eyck a.a.O., S. 95.
[2] Ernst II., *Aus meinem Leben*, Berlin 1887, I.S. 273ff.

Der kühnste aller aufgestellten Pläne stammte ebenfalls aus dem Coburger Kreis, nämlich von Baron Stockmar, und fand sich in seiner 'Denkschrift an die Konstituierende Deutsche National-versammlung' vom April 1848.[1] Danach sollte nur ein Fürst mit starker Hausmacht zum Kaiser erhoben werden, dem zugleich aber die Verwandlung seiner Hausmacht in Reichsland zugemutet wurde. Das hätte für Preußen bedeutet, daß es im Einheitsstaat aufgegangen wäre. Der preußische Gesandte von Bunsen war zeitweilig für diesen Plan, um seinem König gegen die aufsässige Berliner Nationalversammlung beizuspringen. Indessen wies der König schon am 17. Juni 1848 diesen Plan freundlich zurück. Er wurde ihm später nochmals von Frankfurt aus entgegengetragen unter dem Vorzeichen eines konstitutionellen Liberalismus, der gegen den gemeinsamen demokratischen Gegner umgebildet war und eine populäre Allianz von Fürsten und liberalen Politikern zustande bringen sollte.[2] Der Plan scheiterte daran, daß Preußen seine Staatspersönlichkeit nicht aufgeben wollte und konnte. Wahlkaisertum Alberts und Reichslandidee Stockmars sollten den Fürsten den Bundesstaat schmackhaft machen. Elemente daraus lassen sich in der Reichsgründung von 1870 wiedererkennen.

Das Grundanliegen Alberts klammerte sich vernünftigerweise nicht an bestimmte Konzeptionen, sondern war allgemeiner Natur. Es begnügte sich im Grunde mit Beachtung der Rechts-staatlichkeit und der öffentlichen Meinung. Er schrieb am 21. August 1849 an Bunsen: 'Existiert ein Rechtszustand in Deutsch-land und eine Regierung, die in ein Verhältnis von Wechsel-wirkung zu der öffentlichen Meinung gestellt ist, dann wird es Zeit sein, an eine europäische Politik zu denken. Ehe dies der Fall ist, wird jedes Auftreten auf dem europäischen Felde nur neue Elemente der Störung in den inneren Regenerationsprozeß wer-fen.'[3] Nach dem Scheitern des Werks der Paulskirche war der König von Preußen Alberts ständiger Briefpartner und dann

[1] vgl. Meinecke a.a.O., S. 314f.   [2] ebd. S. 334.
[3] Archiv Windsor, I, 16.34 n.; Eyck a.a.O., S. 148/9.

immer stärker Prinz Wilhelm. Er schrieb ihm 1852: 'Wir sind die einzigen Vertreter liberaler und konstitutioneller Institutionen in Europa und müssen uns auf den vollsten Haß von Seiten der reaktionären Regierungen gefaßt machen, die aber doch zuweilen eine dunkel Ahnung zu haben scheinen, daß das Beispiel Englands doch endlich obsiegen wird.'[1] Offenbar war die enge Beziehung zu Wilhelm zur Achse seiner weiteren politischen Konzeptionen geworden.

Gerade daraus erwuchs eine Staatskrise in Preußen, die uns Indikator für die Chancen sind, die Alberts Politik damals hatte. Sie hängt unmittelbar mit dem Krimkrieg 1854–56 zusammen. Hier nahm Albert eine vermittelnde Haltung ein; er durchschaute den russischen Expansionismus ebenso klar wie die türkischen Pressionen gegen die Christen. Es galt den Zaren in Schach zu halten, ohne den Einfluß an der Pforte zu verlieren. Albert plädierte deswegen für eine gemeinsame europäische Politik, die der christlichen Bevölkerung unter dem Sultan Rechte sichern sollte, ohne dabei einem einzelnen Staat die alleinige Mitrede in Konstantinopel zu überlassen. Er wandte sich scharf gegen russische Protektorats- und Aufteilungspläne und hielt einen Zusammenschluß der West- und Mittelmächte für eine absolute Notwendigkeit. Er sah die Dinge ganz vom moralischen Standpunkt aus und hielt den Krimkrieg für einen Kreuzzug um der guten Sache willen, nämlich um das öffentliche Recht Europas zu fördern und dabei die Türkei in das europäische Konzert der Mächte einzugliedern. Dies mußte Preußen aber an die Westmächte verpflichten.[2] Zugleich hielt Albert nunmehr die Loslösung Preußens und Österreichs von Rußland für eine Vorbedingung, um die deutsche und die italienische Frage lösen zu können. Der Krimkrieg stellte offensichtlich die Weichen für die Zukunft des Kontinents. Dazu bedurfte es in erster Linie eines Gesin-

[1] George Gillespie, 'Prinzgemahl Albert – ein Überblick', *Jahrbuch der Coburger Landesstiftung*, 1971, S. 84; vgl. H. R. Fischer-Aue, *Die Deutschlandpolitik des Prinzgemahls Albert von England 1848–52*, Coburg u. Hannover, 1953.
[2] Eyck a.a.O., S. 287/88.

nungswandels in Berlin, der nicht vom Kabinett Manteuffel, wohl aber vom König oder vom Prinzen Wilhelm kommen konnte.

Der Krimkrieg schien den Coburgern die große Chance zuzuspielen, die sie brauchten, um Mitteleuropa in den westlichen Zusammenhang zu integrieren. Die ganze liberale öffentliche Meinung Westeuropas war für einen Anschluß Preußens an die Westmächte, auch Prinz Wilhelm und das neue Preußische Wochenblatt unter Bethmann Hollweg, desgleichen Kriegsminister von Bonin und der Gesandte von Bunsen. Diese beiden hatten sich schon offen gegen Rußland ausgesprochen, mußten aber deswegen gehen. König Friedrich Wilhelm IV. trat nämlich für strikte Neutralität ein. Das führte zu einem ernsten Konflikt. Der Prinz ließ sich als Sturmbock und Wortführer gegen den König gebrauchen, der seinerseits an seiner deklarierten Neutralitätspolitik ohne Einschränkung festhielt. Die tiefgehenden Meinungsverschiedenheiten streiften schon an Rebellion.[1] Der Hinweis Wilhelms auf die gleichlaufenden Ansichten König Léopolds ließ zudem erkennen, woher der Wind wehte.[2] Der Vorfall war nichts Geringeres als eine Thronfolgerkrise, die nach harten Worten gütlich beigelegt wurde. Diese preußische Neutralitätspolitik nötigte bald auch zur Trennung von Österreich (am 2. Dezember 1854) und wurde von Bismarck im Sinne des Königs ins Werk gesetzt.[3] Das brachte dann allerdings Preußen auf der Friedenskonferenz in Paris 1856 ins Hintertreffen.

Die preußische Staatskrise von 1854 macht deutlich, wie groß die realen Chancen für eine Westwendung Preußens damals waren. Die Verlobung des Prinzen Friedrich Wilhelm mit der Royal Princess 1855, dann deren Heirat 1858 und der Beginn der 'Neuen Aera' 1858 verhießen einen liberalen Frühling für Preußen.

Diese Krise hatte noch ein bedeutungsvolles Nachspiel, insofern König Friedrich Wilhelm seinen Nachfolger zur Aufhebung der Verfassung und zum Octroi einer anderen Verfassung unter

---

[1] vgl. Peter Rassow, *Der Konflikt König Friedrich Wilhelms IV. mit dem Prinzen von Preußen im Jahre 1854. Eine preußische Staatskrise*, Wiesbaden 1961, S. 758f; 734f.
[2] Brief Wilhelms vom 7 Aug. 1854 ebd.   [3] Rassow a.a.O., S. 759.

Wahrung des monarchischen Prinzips verpflichten wollte. Albert riet damals seinem künftigen Schwiegersohn, sich als 'Treuhänder der nächsten Generation' zu betrachten und beim Bruch einer beschworenen Verfassung kein unbeteiligter Zuschauer zu bleiben. Er schlug ferner in einem Schreiben vom 6. November 1855 dem Prinzen Wilhelm vor, gegen das Vermächtnis seines Bruders 'feierlichen Protest' im Sinne einer 'Rechtsverwahrung' einzulegen, im Namen aller, 'deren Rechte ich als für unzertrennlich mit den meinigen ansehen würde: die meiner Nation und meines Volkes'.[1] Als Prinzregent hat Wilhelm das Vermächtnis des Königs seinem Hause bekannt gemacht und trotzdem den vorgeschriebenen Eid auf die Verfassung am 26. Oktober 1858 geleistet. Kaiser Wilhelm II. hat dann 1888 bei seinem Regierungsantritt das Vermächtnis seines Oheims den Flammen übergeben und sein Königtum damit 'für alle Zeiten' auf konstitutionelle Grundlagen gestellt.

Als Prinzregent und dann als König von Preußen sprach Wilhelm von der Verantwortlichkeit des Königs in den Worten Alberts. Mit der 'Neuen Aera' und dem liberalen Ministerium unter Fürst Karl-Anton von Hohenzollern-Sigmaringen sowie dem Regierungsprogramm vom 8. November 1858 schien der liberale Systemwechsel vollzogen zu sein. Albert gab zu Wilhelm seiner Freude Ausdruck, 'eine Kontinentalmacht zu sehen, welche sich ganz auf das Gebiet der Rechtlichkeit und Billigkeit stellen will, und so ein höchst wichtiges korrektives Element in der großen Intrigenpolitik des Kontinents werden wird.'[2] Er schickte sogar am 4. Mai 1859 ein längeres Memorandum zu Wilhelm,[3] wonach Preußen für sich allein eines Stützpunktes von außen bedürfe und deshalb – von Deutschland getrennt – keine Großmacht sein könne. In Zusammenhang aber mit Deutschland und an dessen Spitze sei es eine Großmacht; es brauche keinen Alliierten, wenn es mit Deutschland identifiziert werde. Alberts

[1] zit.n.Eyck a.a.O., S. 299/300.
[2] 26. Nov. 1858, Archiv Windsor, I, 31.30; Eyck a.a.O., S. 296.
[3] Archiv Windsor, J, 19. 27; Eyck a.a.O., S. 297.

gutgemeinte Ratschläge rissen nicht ab, wobei Preußen nur als 'Champion für die Volksrechte' seine Führungsrolle übernehmen könne[1] aber, so heißt es plötzlich in einem Brief an König Léopold vom 4. Juli 1861, es werde am Widerwillen der höheren Klassen, vor allem an der Junkerpartei und der Bürokratenpartei scheitern.[2]

Viele Briefe vom Todesjahr 1861 zeigen Enttäuschung und Zweifel. Was war geschehen? – Das preußische Angebot an Österreich im Krieg gegen Italien 1859 und die damit verbundene preußische Mobilmachung mit Aufmarsch am Oberrhein hatten die Mängel der preußischen Armee trotz Wiedereinführung der dreijährigen Dienstzeit 1856 offensichtlich gemacht. Der plötzliche Waffenstillstand von Villafranca brachte Preußen in eine unvorhergesehene Isolierung und in diplomatische Schwierigkeiten. Das wurde den Ratschlägen Alberts angekreidet, die immer nur von Abwarten und Neutralität redeten. Die Antwort Wilhelms war eine Heeresreform, die mit der Berufung des Generals Albrecht von Roon als Kriegsminister anstelle von Bonin am 3. Dezember 1859 eingeleitet wurde. Daran schloß sich im Mai 1860 ein Reformvorschlag Wilhelms in Bezug auf die Bundeskriegsverfassung an, den der Deutsche Bund unter Führung Österreichs ablehnte. Nur Ernst II., regierender Herzog von Coburg, sowie Waldeck und Altenburg unterstellten ihre Truppenkontingente dem Vorschlag entsprechend dem preußischen Oberbefehl. Schlimmer war, daß sich in der Zweiten Preußischen Kammer, dem Abgeordnetenhaus, entschlossene Gegenkräfte sammelten. Schon im Juni 1861 bildete sich in Preußen eine radikale liberale Partei, die Fortschrittspartei, die auf Konfliktkurs ging, das Ende des Altliberalismus einläutete und bei den Wahlen am 5. November 1861 100 von 120 Sitzen im preußischen Abgeordnetenhaus errang. An eine normale Lösung des Heereskonfliktes entsprechend den Vorstellungen Roons und Wilhelms war also

[1] Schr. an den Kronprinzen von Preußen am 1. Mai 1861, Archiv Windsor, I, 36.1.
[2] Albert an Léopold am 4. Juli 1861, Archiv Windsor, I, 36.57.

nicht mehr zu denken. Der Verfassungskonflikt war damit vorpro-grammiert, der alle Pläne Alberts zerschlug.

In den Sommer der Neuen Aera fuhr ein eisiger Frost. Wilhelm wollte abdanken, als der Heereskonflikt zu einem Verfassungs-konflikt wurde, abdanken zugunsten des Kronprinzen Friedrich. Das wäre der Triumph von Coburg geworden. Der Traum Alberts hätte sich erfüllt. Ganz Europa hatte sich auf liberalen Fuß gestellt. Der Kronprinz ergriff nicht die Chance, und Bismarck nahm das Heft in die Hand. Albert hätte die Chance sicherlich wahrgenommen. Aber er war schon am 14. Dezember 1861 gestorben. Er erlebte also nicht den Umschwung der Weltverhält-nisse, der sich in Amerika, Asien und Indien anbahnte und dem kommerziellen und konstitutionellen Liberalismus Schranken setzte. Vor allem auch nicht die Abwendung Preußens vom Ver-fassungsliberalismus zum Nationalliberalismus und zum Natio-nalismus hin.

Es gab noch Nachwirkungen jenes Honoratiorenliberalismus wie etwa die 'Rechtsverwahrung', die Kronprinz Friedrich in seiner Danziger Rede von 1863 gegen Bismarcks Pressever-ordnung nach den Ratschlägen Alberts von 1855 einlegte; oder die konstitutionelle Selbstverpflichtung Wilhelms II. 1888; oder die Versöhnungspolitik Bismarcks und des Kronprinzen in Nikolsburg 1866. Aber im ganzen war die Epoche zuende!

Das letzte Eingreifen Alberts in die Politik am 30. November 1861 bereits von seinem Sterbebett aus war bezeichnenderweise ein Akt der Versöhnung und des Ausgleichs von weltpolitischer Bedeutung. Es handelte sich um den Jacinto-Zwischenfall am 7. November 1861. Die 'San Jacinto', ein amerikanisches Kriegs-schiff der Nordstaaten hatte auf hoher See von einem britischen Postdampfer zwei Abgesandte der Südstaaten, die nach England bzw. Frankreich gehen sollten, heruntergeholt. Die Regierung Palmerston verlangte in ultimativer Form Genugtuung für diesen Bruch des Seerechts und bereitete kriegerische Maßnahmen vor. Albert indessen schwächte den Text der Depesche nach Washington beträchtlich ab, indem er der Hoffnung Ausdruck gab, daß der amerikanische Kapitän ohne Instruktionen gehandelt hätte und die beiden Gefangenen umgehend britischem Schutz unterstellen würde. Staatssekretär Seward nahm den Ball auf und sagte zu, daß die USA selbstverständlich entsprechend den britischen Vorschlägen verfahren würden, da Amerika hiermit nur dem genüge, was es selbst immer verlangt habe. Schon am 1. Dezember war die Affaire ausgeräumt,[1] und damit eine unabdingbare Voraussetzung für einen aussichtsreichen Kampf der Nordstaaten gegen den Süden, nämlich die Neutralität Englands, geschaffen.

Die Bedeutung Prinz Alberts für die europäische Politik ist in den Augen vieler Nachgeborener unterschätzt worden,[2] weil viel Tinte und Papier auf Familienpolitik, Denkschriften, Beratung und Information verschwendet wurde, ohne eine Weichenstellung nach den Wünschen des konstitutionellen Liberalismus durchzusetzen. In der Tat erscheint Alberts europäische Politik als verlorene Liebesmüh' am ungeeigneten Objekt. Aber wenn man einer Epoche gerecht werden will, sollte man – mit Fustel de Coulanges und Walter Benjamin zu sprechen – sich aus dem Kopf schlagen, was man vom späteren Verlauf der Geschichte weiß. Auch in diesem Falle soll man die Geschichte 'gegen den Strich bürsten', also mehr auf Karthago sehen als auf Rom, mehr sein Augenmerk auf diejenigen richten, die nicht im Triumphzug des Sieges mitmarschieren und verloren haben oder gescheitert sind.

In Bezug auf die Coburger Politik sind außerdem mancherlei Vorurteile auszuräumen, weil sie hinter den Kulissen oder neben der amtlichen Politik sich abspielte. Bismarcks wegwerfendes Wort von den 'Coburger Intrigen' oder der Verdacht einer 'Coburger Verschwörung' unterschob dunkle Absichten, wo in Wirklichkeit bester Wille und lautere Gesinnung überwogen. Es blieb freilich irritierend, daß das coburgische Plädoyer für einen modernen Konstitutionalismus außerkonstitutionelle und öffent-

---

[1] Southgate a.a.O., S. 489f.   [2] George Gillespie a.a.O., S. 79.

lich nicht verfolgbare Formen und Wege benutzte, also vom Standpunkt des Konstitutionalismus mißbräuchlich war. Das bedeutete jedoch nicht, daß es damit schon absolut oder illusionär gewesen sei. Gewiß war das Spiel abseits der politischen Bühne und unter Nutzung persönlicher Beziehungen ohne Einfluß auf die Öffentlichkeit. Es hing völlig an den daran beteiligten Personen. Deswegen war auch der unerwartete Tod Alberts das Ende einer solchen Politik, zumal auch 'Onkel Léopold', 'Old Palmy', der Baron von Stockmar und andere in den sechziger Jahren starben. Vom 'Coburger Kreis' erlebten nur wenige die Reichsgründung.

Gravierender war gewiß, daß die dahinter stehende Mentalität den Zeitgenossen nicht mehr überzeugend erschien. Die Parolen von Liberalisierung und Konstitutionalisierung hatten nach 1848 an Zündkraft eingebüßt, während die Nationalbewegungen in Mitteleuropa jetzt erst zum Erfolg kamen. Es war für Deutschland ein Verhängnis, daß das liberal-konstitutionelle Anliegen sich nicht – wie Albert es erstrebt hatte – mit dem nationalen Anliegen verbinden konnte. Das lag an unglücklichen Umständen, zumal König Wilhelm I. von Preußen ohne Vorbehalt die konstitutionelle Verpflichtung der Krone anerkannt und beschworen hatte.

Aber der anti-englische Affekt, der sich schon 1848 an der Schleswig-Holstein-Frage entzündet hatte, kam 1864 erneut ins Spiel, trotz der Zurückhaltung der Königin Victoria und der britischen Neutralität. Die Annexionspolitik Bismarcks gegen Schleswig-Holstein und gegen Hannover konnte indessen von London nicht gutgeheißen werden. Das deutsche Nationalgefühl entzündete sich an den Waffenerfolgen und verband sich mit einer Verfassungsverdrossenheit, die dem deutschen politischen Liberalismus das Überleben schwer machte. Die Konstitutionalisierung Preußens blieb ungenügend.

Diese Diskreditierung des westlichen Liberalismus in Deutschland war ein Unglück, aber keineswegs unabwendbar. Die Idee Alberts von einem modernen Konstitutionalismus, überparteilich,

jenseits der Konfessionen und Klassen, unter dem Dach europäischer Regulative aus Menschenrecht, Völkerrecht und Freiheit
zur Selbstbestimmung, in freier Vereinbarung gefunden und als
gesamteuropäische Notwendigkeit anerkannt, das war für die
Coburger eine Art Glaubensartikel, unentbehrlich für den Fort-
bestand Europas.

Was Albert wollte, war nicht seine persönliche Marotte sondern
lag auf der Linie der früheren britischen Europapolitik. Schon der
jüngere Pitt dachte an den Aufbau eines allgemeinen und mit
Zwinggewalt ausgestatteten System des öffentlichen Rechts, das
aus der kollektiven Verantwortlichkeit der Fürsten für Europa
entstehen sollte. Ein wichtiger Schritt dahin war ja schon die
Schaffung Belgiens. Es war die Idee der Coburger, daß ein solches
System einer konstitutionellen Basis in allen beteiligten Staaten
bedurfte, um eine öffentliche Meinung ganz Europas zustande zu
bringen. Die Ansätze der Wiener Friedensordnung von 1815
mußten nur zu einem europäisch verbindlichen konstitutionellen
Regulativ fortentwickelt werden. Das war die höchste politische
Idee der Coburger, die gemeinsame europäische Politik er-
möglichen sollte. Es war eine große Idee und auch eine typische
Idee für das 'Age of Improvement'.

Politik war für sie Weltverbesserung! Wie einfach war das! –
Hier war Albert vielleicht wirklich ein großer Mann, jedenfalls
aber ein großer Organisator, der über die Politik hinaus die
Forderungen und Konsequenzen des Industrialismus, der Massen-
gesellschaft, der Arbeitswelt, des Welthandels, des Bildungs-
wesens und der Wissenschaft durchschaute und im Namen des
Fortschritts mannigfache Initiativen ergriff, die schon für die
Gesellschaft von morgen gedacht waren, wobei nicht nur an die
Weltausstellung von 1851, die Förderung von Kunst und Wissenschaft sondern etwa auch an die Arbeiterwohnsiedlungsprojekte
in Battersea – sogar schon mit Wasserklosetts! – zu denken ist.

Hier sollte heute nur die politische Seite betont werden und zum
Ausdruck kommen, daß Alberts Politik eine echte Chance für

Europa und ein 'gemeines Weltrecht der Kulturstaaten' (v. Holtzendorff) bot. Politik in seinem Sinne fand nur unter zivilisierten Ländern statt und war ihm nur vorstellbar als integre Tätigkeit von Gentlemen, die sich als Treuhänder fühlten und bereit waren, ihre Politik einem Verfahren zu unterwerfen, das die Normen der Verfassung mit den Wünschen der öffentlichen Meinung und nach den Regeln einer europäischen Friedensordnung in Einklang zu bringen verstand. Das war gewiß viktorianisch und gewiß auch 'zu schön um wahr zu sein!' Daß es anders kam, spricht nicht gegen Prinz Albert, der unser geschichtliches Interesse verdient, das in seinem Ausnahmefall mit unserem menschlichen Interesse identisch ist.

LÉOPOLD I,
VICTORIAS ONKEL

JACQUES WILLEQUET

WÄHREND des Ersten Weltkrieges, in einer Zeit wo er allgemein als Nationalheld verherrlicht wurde, sagte König Albert von Belgien einmal: 'Eigentlich bin ich kein echter Belgier. Ich gehöre zu einer fremden Familie, die mit dem belgischen Volke ein Bündnis geschlossen hat.' Dieser Satz ist für die ganze Dynastie maßgebend, diese Dynastie, die 1831 mit Léopold I. von Sachsen-Coburg begann. Kein echter Belgier, sagte er? Nun, Alberts Vater war eine Mischung von Sachsen-Coburg und Orléans, seine Mutter eine v. Hohenzollern-Sigmaringen, die zwei französische Großmütter hatte, tadellos französisch, englisch, italienisch, deutsch und noch dazu schwäbisch sprach. Alberts nächsten Verwandten hatten die verschiedensten Nationalitäten: eine bayerische Gemahlin, ein rumänischer Onkel, eine österreichische Tante, französische und preussische Schwäger und, darüber hinaus, Engländer, Portugiesen, Italiener, Bulgaren usw. Nationalstaaten in Europa sind eine Neuheit des XIX. Jahrhunderts und die Coburger, wie alle Fürstenhäuser, haben weit über diese hinaus zurückweichende Würzeln, deren Traditionen in aristokratisch-kosmopolitischen Europa des Vormärz oder des Ancien Régime liegen. Diese Feststellung ist allerdings eine Selbstverständlichkeit, aber sie gehört zu den vielen Selbstverständlichkeiten, die man leicht übersieht, und über die man hie und da etwas nachdenken muß, wenn man den Nagel auf dem Kopfe treffen will – sonst bleibt manches unverständlich: so z.B. Léopolds III. Unterhaltung mit Hitler 1940, Alberts Verzweiflung

133

um Europa während des Ersten Weltkrieges, viele Charakterzüge seines Vorgängers Léopold II. und schließlich unser Léopold I. Und was ist dieses Bündnis zwischen dem Herrscherhause und dem Volke? Es heißt belgische Verfassung, auf welche jeder König bei jedem Thronwechsel einen Eid ablegen muß, den er auch peinlichst respektiert. In den letzten 150 Jahren sind die Beziehungen zwischen König und Volk nicht immer reibungslos gewesen, aber für den Historiker kommen diese Schwierigkeiten immer auf dieselbe Feststellung zurück: die Verfassung, ein Bündnis zwischen zwei gleichgestellten Partnern – das Herrscherhaus auf der einen Seite, die Belgier auf der anderen.

Léopold I., Gründer der Dynastie, ist also gewiß eine bedeutende belgische Gestalt, aber auch eine große coburgische, britische und europäische Gestalt, deren Hauptzüge ich versuchen werde, zu skizzieren.

Reiche persönliche und politische Erfahrungen hatte der Vierzigjährige schon hinter sich, als er 1831 belgischer König wurde. 1790 in Coburg geboren, hatte er als Jüngling die materiellen Interessen des Fürstentums in seinen Unterhaltungen mit Napoleon verteidigt. Als dieser Versuch scheiterte, wandte er sich Rußland zu, wurde russischer General, nahm an einer Anzahl von Schlachten teil, und hielt 1814 mit dem zaristischen Generalstab seinen Einzug in Paris. Schon hatte er mit den Russen, Preussen und Österreichern eine diplomatische Erfahrung erlangt, jedoch hieß jetzt der eigentliche Sieger Großbritannien: noch im selben Jahr ließ er sich in London nieder. Seine Schwester Victoria war mit ihm eingewandert. Sie heiratete den Duke of Kent, und beide wurden die Eltern der zukünftigen Queen Victoria, während Léopold am 2. Mai 1816 die Kronprinzessin Charlotte heiratete. Ein Jahr später schlugen jedoch seine höchsten Hoffnungen fehl; mit dem Tode seiner jungen Gemahlin gingen zu gleicher Zeit für ihn eine glückliche Ehe und die Prospekte einer politischen Rolle in England zugrunde (als er 1865 starb, hieß sein letztes Wort 'Charlotte', und niemand kann sagen, ob er damit seine erste Gemahlin oder seine Tochter meinte, der er denselben Vornamen gegeben hatte; von dieser Tochter wird später die Rede sein). Er war inzwischen Engländer geworden, zog sich in Claremont zurück, und in dieser Residenz beherbergte er seine Schwester mit ihrem Töchterchen Victoria: die Duchess of Kent hatte auch ihre Gatte verloren, – und es ist für uns wichtig zu erwähnen, daß er von nun an sowohl seine väterliche Liebe der kleinen Victoria widmete, als auch seine politischen Hoffnungen in sie setzte. Zwischen der zukünftigen Queen und ihrem 'dearest Uncle' entflochten sich für das ganze Leben die innigsten Bande des Herzens und des politischen Ehrgeizes, die sich jedoch, wie wir sehen werden, nicht immer reibungslos gestalteten. Zielbewußt aber vorsichtig blieb der hohe Herr in England gewöhnlich ein kluger Beobachter und gelegentlich heimlicher Mitspieler der britischen Politik, und beinahe hätte er 1828–9 die griechische Krone angenommen. Es bleibt dahingestellt, welche mannigfaltigen Gründe ihn schließlich veranlaßten, auf diese hohe Stellung zu verzichten; wahrscheinlich hoffte er, unter den damaligen Umständen doch noch eine gewisse Rolle in England spielen zu können.

Ein Jahr später, im August/September 1830, erhoben sich die Belgier gegen die Holländer; ein Ereignis, dessen 150. Jubiläum dieses Jahr gefeiert wird, und dessen internationale Folgen die damaligen Belgier kaum erfaßten. Man hatte sich weder bei den Belgiern noch bei den Holländern darum befragt, als der Wiener Kongreß sie in einem Vereinigten Königreich der Niederlande zusammengeschlossen hatte. In einem europäischen Gleichgewichtssystem mußte ein fester Riegel an der nordfranzösischen Grenze gezogen werden, um nach 23 Jahren Angriffskriegen gegen Europa eventuelle erneute Abenteuer revolutionärer oder napoleonischer Art abzuschrecken. Schon die Juli-revolution in Paris hatte die konservativen Mächte sehr beunruhigt, aber Gott sei Dank war der neue Franzosenkönig Louis-Philippe ein friedlicher Mensch. Man begann sich mit ihm abzufinden, als jetzt die

Belgier einen Barrikadenbürgerkrieg und eine liberale Revolution losließen. Und in ihrer Naivität gingen die Belgier so weit, daß sie versuchten, Louis-Philippe zu kompromittieren, und einen seiner Söhne als König wählten! Das stand natürlich außer Frage. In einer Londoner Konferenz versammelten sich die damaligen fünf Großmächte Europas – Großbritannien, Frankreich, Preußen, Österreich und Rußland – um eine friedliche Lösung zu finden. Louis-Philippe lehnte selbstverständlich die Krone ab, die seinem Sohne vorgeschlagen worden war, und die Frage wurde in einer wohlbekannten Weise gelöst: den Belgiern wurde ihre Unabhängigkeit gegönnt, weil es nicht anders ging, aber unter der strikten Bedingung, daß der neue Staat ewig neutral bliebe – eine Neutralität, die natürlich gegen Frankreich gerichtet wurde.

Und wiederum stellte sich die Frage: welcher König für Belgien? In dieser Zeit, in der es noch kein geeinigtes deutsches Reich gab, war der Deutsche Bund eine Gottgesegnete Quelle, woraus man nach Belieben neue Könige für neue Nationen schöpfen konnte: Fürsten, die nicht zu eng an eine der Hauptmächte Europas gebunden waren. Als ehemaliger russischer General war Léopold von Sachsen-Coburg am zaristischen Hof persona grata; mit den Habsburgern hatte er die besten Beziehungen, und Preußen hatte keine Bedenken. Die englischen Gefühle waren mehr gemischt: zwar war er Engländer geworden, aber gerade deswegen fürchteten manche seinen allzu großen Einfluß auf seine Nichte, die Kronprinzessin Victoria, besonders wenn er in England verbleiben sollte. In Brüssel wäre er perfekt an seinem Platze. Zudem wurde auch noch eine raffinierte Lösung gefunden: durch Léopolds Heirat mit einer Tochter Louis-Philippes würde man erstens dem Franzosenkönig einen Gefallen tun und das Gleichgewicht der fünf Mächte stärken, aber zweitens denselben Franzosenkönig auch davon abschrecken, irgendetwas gegen das Königreich seines Schwiegersohnes zu unternehmen. Am 21. Juli 1831 hielt Léopold I. seinen feierlichen Einzug in Brüssel, legte seinen Eid auf die Verfassung ab und verband sich somit mit der neuen Nation.

Ich glaube, daß die Haupteigenschaft einer Abhandlung, so bescheiden sie auch sei, die Klarheit sein muß. Gerne hätte ich jetzt diesen Léopold in seinen verschiedenen Erscheinungen separat skizziert: der Belgier, der Coburger, der Deutsche, der Europäer, der Diplomat, der Onkel vieler Neffen und Nichten. Diese Methode erwies sich als glatt unmöglich. Wann ist der hohe Herr romantisch und wann ein kalter Politiker, wo endet bei ihm das Herz und wann kalkuliert er, wo und wie gestalten sich seine Hintergedanken und seine weitgespannten Pläne? Alles unternimmt er zu gleicher Zeit, überall hat er ein Auge, zielbewußt und zäh verfolgt er die verschiedensten Kombinationen, und seine wirklichen Beweggründe sind nicht immer auf den ersten Blick erkennbar. Dem Historiker bleibt also nichts anderes übrig, als chronologisch sein Handeln und Wirken zu verfolgen, und vielleicht erst am Ende etwas Klares in dieses Leben zu bringen.

Für die Ostmächte – Preußen, Österreich und Rußland – war und blieb er nach 1830 ein Barrikadenkönig, der seine Krone einer Revolution zu verdanken hatte. Mit Zähigkeit trachte er danach, ganz besonders Metternichs Achtung zu gewinnen, das heißt, als Anhänger und Verteidiger des Konservatismus zu erscheinen. Konservieren hieß beibehalten, und was zunächst verstärkt und beibehalten werden mußte, hieß Belgien – aber dafür mußte er auch in London und Paris den größtmöglichsten Einfluß erreichen. Die belgische Unabhängigkeit hing schließlich vom Frieden zwischen diesen zwei Westmächten ab; sollten sie wiederum gegeneinander Krieg führen, so würde dies erstens auf belgischem Boden geschehen, wie so oft in der Geschichte, und höchstwahrscheinlich würde zweitens seine eigene Krone zugrundegehen.

Viele Nichten und Neffen hatte er, die sehr nutzvoll sein konnten – und an erster Stelle Victoria. Seine große Liebe für Victoria stand gewiß außer Frage, ebenso wie die Gefühle der jungen Dame für ihren 'dearest Uncle'. Victorias Tagebuch zeugt absolut dafür, und das zärtliche Interesse des Onkels für ihre Erziehung war gewiß einwandfrei aufrichtig – aber die Nichte war auch ein Trumpf in seiner weitblickenden Politik. Unzählige gute Ratschläge gab er ihr, die auch freudig angenommen wurden. Besonders pochte er darauf, daß die junge Dame Geschichtsbücher lesen sollte. Schon waren seine Hintergedanken klar, und eine ganz bestimmte Zukunft hatte er in Sicht. Eine persönliche Niederlage hatte er mit dem Tode seiner ersten Frau erlitten; das konnte wiedergutgemacht werden, die Stellung eines englischen Prinzgemahls mußte in Coburger Hand bleiben, und sein Neffe Albert war dafür der geeignete Mann.

Auch schien die Sache anfangs zu klappen. Albert fuhr nach England, Victoria war begeistert: 'I must thank you, my beloved Uncle, for the prospect of great happiness you have contributed to give me, in the person of dear Albert...He possesses every quality that could be desired to render me perfectly happy. He is so sensible, so kind and so good, and so amiable too. He has, besides, the most pleasing and delightful exterior and appearance you can possibly see' (7. Juni 1836).

Aber zur gleichen Zeit hatte der König noch andere Eisen im Feuer. Aus seinem Zauberkästchen zog er einen anderen Neffen, Ferdinand von Sachsen-Coburg, 19 Jahre alt, der die 17jährige Dona Maria von Portugal heiratete. Die Lage war dort sehr gespannt. Reaktionäre, Gemäßigte und Linksliberale stritten sich, Anhänger mehr oder weniger fortschrittlicher Verfassungen erhoben sich gegeneinander. Dem jungen Ehepaar mußte geholfen werden. Zwei begabte belgische Diplomaten – Van de Weyer und Goblat – wurden nach Lissabon geschickt, Van de Weyer mußte zwischen englischem und französischem Einfluß manövrieren, er unterstützte einen Staatsstreich und das genau 6 Jahre alte Belgien sendete ein Freiwilligenkorps, das sich in die portugiesischen Angelegenheiten mischte...Erstaunlich, für eine junge Nation! Gerne hätte Léopold zur gleichen Zeit dasselbe Spiel in Madrid versucht, wo die Königin Maria-Christine mit den Carlisten zu tun hatte, aber in diesem Falle kam ihm Metternich schroff dazwischen.

Léopold I, Victorias Onkel

Ein Jahr später bestieg Victoria den Thron, und schon hatte ihr der König am 15. Juni 1837 geschrieben: 'My beloved Child...My object is you should be no one's tool, and though young, and naturally not yet experienced, your good natural sense and the truth of your character will, with faithful and proper advice, get you very well through the difficulties of your future position' – worauf Victoria sofort antwortete: 'My dearly beloved Uncle... Your advice is most excellent, and you may depend upon it I shall make use of it, and follow it.' Wie wir sehen werden, folgte sie auch bald diesen guten Ratschlägen – aber nicht wie der gute Onkel sie gemeint hatte. Und einige Tage später nach diesem Briefwechsel: 'My dear Child...May Heaven assist you, and may I have the happiness of being able to be of use to you, and to contribute to those successes in your new career for which I am so anxious' (23. Juni) – und sofort die Antwort: 'My dearly beloved Uncle, though I have an immense deal of business to do (danke ich Ihnen herzlich)...Your advice is always of the greatest importance to me.' Na; das werden wir sofort sehen.

Die belgische Frage war nämlich noch nicht ganz abgeschlossen. Nach einem verlorenen Blitzkrieg gegen die Holländer hatten die Belgier 1831 einen von der Londoner Konferenz aufgezwungenen Friedensvertrag unterzeichnet, wonach das heutige Großherzogtum Luxemburg verlorengehen sollte. Der holländische König dagegen hatte seine Unterschrift verweigert, so daß Brüssel sich daran gewöhnt hatte, diese Provinz weiter zu verwalten. Nun erklärte plötzlich, im März 1838, Wilhelm von Oranien seine Bereitwilligkeit, diese Endlösung zu akzeptieren, was natürlich Belgien arg verstimmte. Wäre es nicht doch möglich eine Formel zu finden, die es erlaubt hätte, die belgischen Grenzen beim Status quo zu lassen? Léopolds innere Glaubwürdigkeit wurde bedroht, er brauchte dringend Victorias Unterstützung, und man kann nur bewundern, mit welcher peinlichen Vorsicht er nach London um Hilfe rief:

All I want from your kind Majesty is, that you will occasionally express to your Ministers, and particularly to good Lord Melbourne, that, as far as it is compatible with the interests of your own dominions, you do not wish that your government should take the lead in such measures as might in a short time bring on the destruction of this country, as well as of your uncle and his family.

worauf Victoria am 10. Juni 1838 antwortete:

I perfectly understand and feel that your position with respect to all these affairs is very difficult and trying, and the feelings of your subjects are far from unnatural; yet I sincerely hope that you will use the great influence you possess over the minds of the leading men in Belgium, to mitigate discontent and calm irritation, and procure acquiescence to whatever arrangements may ultimately be found inevitable. The Treaty of November 1831 was perhaps not so advantageous to the Belgians as one could have wished, yet...this Treaty having been ratified, it is become binding.

Ein recht unangenehmer Schlag für Léopold, der seine Glaubwürdigkeit gegenüber den Zentralmächten bedroht sah. 'I must say', schrieb er verbittert, 'it hurt me more in my English capacity than in my Belgian, as I came to this country from England, and was chosen for this very reason.'

Eine Zeitlang blieben die zärtlichen Verhältnisse also etwas verdorben, und wir besitzen, am 8. Dezember 1839, folgende Äußerung Victorias in einem Briefe an Albert: 'I have received to-day an ungracious letter from Uncle Léopold. He appears to me to be nettled because I no longer ask for his advice, but dear Uncle is given to believe that he must rule the roost everywhere.'

Diese Verstimmung war jedoch sehr kurz. Bald sollte Léopold einen ersten großen Sieg feiern: die Heirat seines Neffen Alberts – und, nach dieser Heirat, die Wiederherstellung, wenn auch oft auf indirekter Weise, seines Einflusses auf Victoria. So einfach ging jetzt die Sache nicht. Victoria hatte Albert etwas aus den Augen verloren, und manche dachten in England: eine Coburger Mutter, ein Coburger Onkel, muß auch noch unsere Königin einen Coburger Gatten nehmen? 'I should like to know', schrieb Léopold, 'what harm the Coburg family has done to England?' Ende gut, alles gut: man weiß, wie dieses große Unternehmen 1840 schließlich gelang, zum Glücke Victorias, und zur immensen Genugtuung ihres Onkels.

Dieser Erfolg kam zur rechten Zeit: dunkle Wolken schwebten über dem Nahen Osten. In Ägypten hatte sich Mehemet Ali gegen seinen Sultan erhoben und hatte Syrien erobert. Die Russen hatten die Gelegenheit nicht verpaßt, um ihren Einfluß im Osmanischen Reich zu erweitern und die Dardanellen zu bedrohen. Hinter dem Sultan standen Österreich und ganz besonders Großbritannien, und das aus zwei Gründen: erstens mußte vor Rußland ein Riegel geschoben werden, aber zweitens, was ebenso wichtig war, unterstützte Frankreich Mehemet Ali, und hoffte, sich in einem großägyptischen Raum eine dominierende Stellung zu sichern. Es durchschnitt in einer total unannehmbaren Weise den Weg nach Indien.

Eine erstaunlich falsche Ansicht, die wohl auf J. J. Rousseau zurückzuführen ist, herrscht bis heute noch im republikanischen Frankreich: die Völker seien von Natur aus friedlich, und die Könige gefährliche Kriegsstifter. Wie anders sah besonders im XIX. Jahrhundert die Wirklichkeit aus! Die friedliche Lösung dieser gefährlichen Krise von 1840 hat Europa seinen Herrscherhäusern zu verdanken – und besonders dem König der Belgier. Léopold I. hatte noch mehr als alle anderen einen guten Grund dafür: die Hauptgaranten der belgischen Unabhängigkeit waren Großbritannien mit seiner Nichte Victoria, und Frankreich mit seinem Schwiegervater Louis-Philippe. Ein Krieg zwischen den beiden hätte zum Ende Belgiens führen können. Außerdem – dieses sei nebenbei bemerkt – war gerade der eifrige Coburger damit beschäftigt, sein Familiennetz noch weiter zu stricken: eine doppelte Heirat seiner Nichte Victoria von Sachsen-Coburg mit dem Herzog von Nemours, und seines Neffen August mit Clementine von Orléans!

Sofort bemühte er sich darum, in Wiesbaden mit Metternich anzuknüpfen, um auf dessen weiche Stelle einen Druck auszuüben: der Frieden, argumentierte er, sei konservativ, nur der Krieg sei revolutionär. Soviele Katastrophen wären seit 1793 aus dem republikanischen Frankreich gekommen, unbedingt müßte

Louis-Philippe gegen die Dämone des Nationalismus gestärkt werden. 'Wir sind', meinte er, 'die Ärzte am Krankenbett Europas.' Er fuhr nach Wiesbaden, nach Paris, nach London, überall suchte er, denselben mildernden Einfluß auszuüben. Zunächst ohne Resultat: im Juli 1840 wurde ein Vertrag zwischen England, Rußland, Österreich und Preußen geschlossen, der allerdings den Zaren unter Kontrolle brachte, obwohl er in Frankreich als eine Herausforderung erschien. Thiers in Paris, Palmerston in London verfolgten die härtesten Linien, die gefährliche Konstellation der revolutionären Kriege war in einem Schlage wiederhergestellt.

Dieser Vertrag, schrieb er sofort aus Paris an Victoria, habe hier einen 'very disastrous effect' verursacht, 'whose consequences may be very serious...and may affect everything in Europe if the mistake is not corrected and moderated'. 'I do give these affairs my most serious attention', antwortete die Queen, jedoch sei es klar, daß die Franzosen 'have put themselves in this unfortunate state'. Palmerston, bemerkte der König am 2. Oktober 1840,

likes to put his foot on their necks. Now, no statesman must triumph over an enemy that is not quite dead, because people forget a real loss, a real misfortune, but they won't forget an insult!...L'union de l'Angleterre et de la France est la base du repos du monde...[Louis Philippe's courage and firmness] are worthy of kinder treatment from the European Powers than he has received.

Kurz, aus den Briefen Victorias geht hervor, daß sie sich von Palmerston distanzierte und ihr Bestes tat, um ihn auf 'more reasonable' (16. Oktober 1840) Wege zu bringen, während Léopold sich auch in Paris darum bemühte, wie aus Theodore Martius' *Life of the Prince Consort* (i, 230) hervorgeht:

He knew England and the way of its people well, and could speak with authority [to Louis-Philippe], when the remonstrances of this country through the usual official channels might not always have commanded a hearing. At the same time his position of perfect neutrality as the Sovereign of a kingdom whose independence was guaranteed by both the Powers, justified him in throwing the weight of his opinion into the scale upon any critical emergency...His judicious intervention was not without its effect in modifying the opinions of King Louis-Philippe, and leading to the abandonment of the warlike attitude which had been assumed by his Government in regard to the Eastern Question.

Der Franzosenkönig entfernte seinen Minister Thiers. Der Ausgleich, der von Léopold vorgeschlagen worden war, wurde auch angenommen, der Friede wurde gerettet, und auch in der Gritchard-Affäre konnte einige Jahre später der Coburger dieselbe mäßigende Rolle spielen.

Das schicksalsvolle Jahr 1848 brachte jedoch Léopold neue Sorgen, aber auch eine sehr große Freude. In allen Hauptstädten Europas entstanden Tumulte und Revolutionen – sein französischer Schwiegervater mußte abdanken –, aber Brüssel blieb vollkommen ruhig und unversehrt: so ruhig, daß der König es sich leisten konnte, dem exilierten Metternich ein Obdach in seiner Residenzstadt zu gewähren. Die ersten, bald gescheiterten Versuche der deutschen und der italienischen Einigung kamen an den Tag. Wenn er es gewollt hätte – und er spielte eine Zeitlang mit dieser Idee – hätte Léopold zum deutschen Kaiser gewählt werden können: man kann nur über das Schicksal Europas träumen, wenn eine so begabte Dynastie, wenn so kluge Herrscher wie ein Léopold II. und ein Albert im XIX. und XX. Jahrhundert an der Spitze der gesamtdeutschen Politik gewesen wären! Jedoch hatte der Coburger für die deutsche Einigung wenig übrig, und vielleicht noch weniger für die italienische.

In den italienischen Ereignissen der Jahre 1848 und 1849 hatte er wiederum Schwierigkeiten mit Palmerston. Zwar waren beide derselben Ansicht und meinten, wie der Engländer sich ausdrückte, 'Wenn Österreich nicht existieren würde, so sollte man es erfinden.' Doch darüber hinaus trennten sich ihre Standpunkte. Palmerston begrüßte eine gewisse italienische Einigung, um desto besser das Habsburger Reich in Ungarn und gegen Rußland zu stärken; Léopold dagegen wollte die Wiener Regierung in den deutschen Angelegenheiten und also auch in der Lombardei unterstützen. Er war gerade dabei, zur Lösung dieser Krise eine europäische Konferenz zu organisieren, die er gerne in Brüssel zusammengerufen hätte, als die Niederlage und die Abdankung des Sardenkönigs Karl-Albert ihn vorläufig von dieser Sorge befreiten.

Und 1857 kam mit dem Staatsstreich in Paris und der Kaiserkrone Napoléon III. eine neue Wende – für Léopold mehr als eine Wende: ein Umschwung. Frankreich wurde für ihn von nun an – auch wenn er hie und da ein schönes Gesicht machte – ein Feindesland, und für seine Krone eine stete Bedrohung. Die Existenz Belgiens war eine Folge der Verträge von 1815, die französischen Könige hatten diese Verträge angenommen, aber ein Napoléon konnte nur deren Zerstörung erstreben.

An Gründen zu belgisch-französischen Schwierigkeiten und Auseinandersetzungen fehlte es auch nicht. Schon persönliche Gründe (Napoléon III. hatte die Erbschaft der Orléans, also der verstorbenen belgischen Königin, beschlagnahmt), aber auch tiefere, so zum Beispiel die unzähligen französischen Opponenten, die sich in Brüssel niedergesetzt hatten und die belgische Pressefreiheit gegen das neue Régime benutzten. Übrigens sind die vielen Annexionspläne des Kaisers bekannt, und Léopold pflegte zu sagen: 'Ich bin hier in der Lage eines Menschen, der in einem Tropenland lebt, eine Schlange in seinem Bett gefunden hat und der nicht weiß, ob er ganz still bleiben muß, oder ob er doch eine Bewegung machen soll, um das gefährliche Tier zu entfernen.' Schon am 5. Dezember 1851 schrieb er an Victoria ironische, aber auch ängstliche Sätze über die 'gloire française', die naturgemäß 'invariably looks to the old frontiers', das heißt zur Rheingrenze, noch über Belgien hinaus. Die Queen verstand den Wink sehr gut: 'Still I think that may be avoided', antwortete sie, und sie fuhr fort: 'Any attempt on Belgium would be a casus belli for us; that you may rely upon.'

Mehr als je mußte sich also Léopold zunächst auf England, aber auch auf den Deutschen Bund stützen. Ständig warnte er Victoria gegen die Franzosen, auch 1855 als die Königin ganz begeistert von ihrer Reise nach Paris zurückkam. Und verschiedene Gesten des Königs sprechen sofort eine deutliche Sprache. Die französische Stütze seines Herrscherhauses war jetzt verloren; er ersetzte sie durch neue Allianzen in Wien. 1853 gab er seinem Sohne, dem zukünftigen Léopold II., die österreichische Erzherzogin Marie-Henriette zur Gemahlin (eine rein politische und wenig glückliche Heirat, aber das war für ihn eine Nebensache). Vier Jahre später gelang es ihm, seine Tochter Charlotte mit dem Habsburger Erzherzog Maximilian zu verloben. Man weiß, und ich werde darauf zurückkommen, wie bald Léopold seinen Ehrgeiz auf seinen Schwiegersohn übertragen sollte, was schließlich in der mexikanischen Affäre dem jungen Kaiser von Mexiko ein tragisches Schicksal bereitete.

Und in Belgien selbst setzte er sich eifrig daran, die nationale Verteidigung neu zu überdenken und umzustellen. Es war illusorisch zu hoffen, daß hunderttausend belgische Soldaten die Franzosen an der Südgrenze schlagen könnten. Höchstens könnten sie sich Schritt für Schritt verteidigen, um sich am Ende in einer großen Festung zu versammeln, wo sie zunächst englische, aber auch andere Hilfen erwarten könnten. Im selben Geiste fing er an, sich mit dem holländischen Nachbarn zu versöhnen. Und kolossale Summen verlangte er vom Parlament, um in Antwerpen die größte Festung Europas zu bauen, wo er sich mit englischer Unterstützung verteidigen könnte. So leicht ging es nicht: die Antwerpner Abgeordneten hatten wenig Lust, ihrer Großstadt die Unannehmlichkeiten eines Kriegsplatzes zu bereiten. Aber doch schaffte er es, und der französische Botschafter in Brüssel berichtete danach in Paris ganz klarsichtig: 'Was der König in Antwerpen machen will, ist nicht so sehr ein Sebastopol als ein Gibraltar...'

Ganz klar ist es, daß Léopold 1860 ein alter Herr von 70 Jahren geworden war, daß seine Gesundheit nicht mehr die beste war, und daß der Einfluß dieses Fürsten des Vormärz geringer wurde. Neue Menschen (Napoléon III., Cavour, Bismarck...) und besonders

neue Ideen gewannen die Oberhand – Ideen, die einen Léopold
völlig befremdeten, und die ihm auch schwere Bedenken
bereiteten, darunter auch der Drang nach einer deutschen
Einigung. So kerndeutsch er auch in seinem Wesen war, betrachtete er diesen Nationalgedanken als eine sentimentale Er-
scheinung, die er absolut nicht billigen konnte, auch wenn er
ehrlich versuchte, sie wenigstens zu verstehen. Schon 1857 hatte er
dem österreichischen Kanzler Schwarzenberg geschrieben: Dieser
Drang habe 'ganz vorzüglich' seinen Ursprung in dem Kampfe
um 1813–14 in den Gemütern, als Antwort auf die herabwürdi-
gende Art, wie die Franzosen die Deutschen als Volk behand-
elten... Es handelt sich also um eine 'praktische Wahrheit'...
'Doch, was über dieses Gefühl hinausgeht, ist voll Schwierigkeit
und selbst Gefahr.'

Bürgerliche Demokratie und Nationalstaat gingen damals
parallel voran, und für keine dieser Erscheinungen hatte der
König viel übrig. Sie kennen Grillparzers Wort: 'Dieser neue Weg
wird uns von der Humanität zur Nationalität, und schließlich zur
Bestialität führen.' Léopold hätte sich diese Formel zu eigen
machen können – ja, er hatte es eigentlich getan, in einem Brief an
den französischen Staatsmann Thiers, der inzwischen sich mit dem
Alter gemäßigt hatte und ein Opponent Napoléon III. geworden
war. Er schrieb 1861: 'Hoffen wir, daß Weisheit und Maß die
Oberhand gewinnen werden. Wenn das nicht der Fall wäre, so
hätten wir Kriege zwischen Nationen, die höchst gefährlich sein
würden, denn es wären Kriege zwischen Fanatikern.' In seiner
Jugendzeit hatte Léopold erlebt, wie die großzügigsten Ideen auch
zu den gewaltigsten Katastrophen führen können: so die französische Revolution, und so die 23 Jahre endloser Kriege und
Qualen für Frankreich und für das gesamte Europa. In seiner
Clausewitz'schen Denkweise, in seinem tiefverwurzelten, christlichen Verantwortungsgefühl, in seiner landesväterlichen Gesinnung schrak er vor nationalistischen Erscheinungen zurück, die
ihm die ärgsten Bedenken bereiteten, sowohl für das ihm anver-

traute Belgien als auch für die Zukunft der abendländischen Zivilisation.

Kein Wunder also, daß ihm das Habsburger Reich als die Hauptstütze des allgemeinen Friedens erschien, und daß er sein Bestes tat, um Ausgleiche zwischen Wien und Belgien zu finden. – 'I fear [Napoleon] is determined on that Italian war', schrieb er im Februar 1859 dem Kaiser Franz-Josef. 'Yet, treaties must be respected, else indeed we return to the old Faustrecht.' Und im Mai schickte er dem Habsburger ein Memorandum mit ausgezeichneten strategischen Ratschlägen, die keiner von ihm verlangt hatte, und die auch nicht ausgeführt wurden. Die österreichische Kriegsführung erwies sich als erbärmlich, und 1861 wurde das italienische Königreich gegründet. Mit Verdruß konnte Léopold als parlamentarisches Staatsoberhaupt nicht abwenden, daß seine Regierung auch dieses neue Reich anerkannte.

Wie kann man erklären, daß dieser 'alte Fuchs', wie ihn Maximilian nannte, sich und seine geliebte Tochter Charlotte in das mexikanische Abenteuer hineinziehen ließ? Gewiß hatte der greise König nicht mehr sein klares Urteil von einst. Immer hatte er, auch für sich selbst, von überseeischen Unternehmungen geträumt, und oft hatte er an den griechischen Thron gedacht, den er in den zwanziger Jahren abgewiesen hatte: 'Belgien war für mich nur Prosa, Griechenland wäre Poesie gewesen', sagte er manchmal. Charlotte, damals 24jährig, hatte von ihm einem endlosen Ehrgeiz geerbt: 'She would go with Max to the end of the world', schrieb er an Victoria. Auch waren die Berichte des belgischen Gesandten in Mexiko irreführend. Jedoch kam der Gedanke einer Kaiserkrone für Maximilian von seinem alten Feinde Napoléon, und Léopold warnte auch seinen Schwiegersohn davor, für den Franzosen nicht die Kastanien aus dem Feuer zu holen.

Einige geschickte Vorbedingungen hatte er gestellt und auch dafür gearbeitet. Nach England war er gefahren und hatte – vergeblich – versucht, dort ein garantiertes Anlehen zu erhalten.

Eifrig hatte er in London und Paris (und auch bei der eigenen Regierung...) für eine Anerkennung der Südstaaten im amerikanischen Bürgerkrieg gewirkt; das Scheitern dieser Vorbedingung hätte ihm die Augen öffnen sollen. Doch hatte er ganz klarsichtig seinem Schwiegersohn geraten, erst die Krone anzunehmen, nachdem Napoléon Mexiko völlig unter seine Verwaltung genommen hatte – und auf der anderen Seite, was widersprüchig war, der Meinung Ausdruck gegeben, man solle doch die Mexikaner selbst ihre Wünsche frei ansprechen lassen. Kurz gesagt, wie sein Biograph Graf Corti sich ausdrückt: 'Er riet zur Vorsicht, gab gute Ratschläge aller Art, aber er riet niemals entschieden ab, obwohl er kein Hehl daraus machte, daß England höchst skeptisch blieb und er dem Franzosenkaiser so sehr mißtraute.'

Im Herbst 1863 ließ er sich von seiner Tochter überzeugen, besprach sogar mit ihr die Grundlinien einer Verfassung für Mexiko. Im Frühjahr entschied sich der Erzherzog, obwohl die anfangs gestellten Bedingungen nicht erfüllt worden waren. Ein Freikorps von etwa tausend Mann war in Belgien geworben worden, theoretisch als Leibgarde für die Kaiserin; praktisch sollte es an zwei Gefechten teilnehmen. Kaiser, Kaiserin und Freikorps verließen Europa. Das Ende des Abenteuers sollte Léopold – ein Glück für ihn – nicht mehr erleben: er starb bekanntlich im Dezember 1865, Maximilian wurde 1867 erschossen, seine inzwischen geisteskrank gewordene Gattin kam nach Europa zurück. Noch 60 Jahre sollte sie leben, um erst 1927 in Brüssel diese Welt zu verlassen.

Ein trauriger Epilog für den greisen hohen Herrn, der so lange als 'Orakel Europas' gegolten hatte. Seit Jahren war er krank, hatte Blasensteine, erduldete furchtbare Qualen und versuchte heldenhaft, hinter Schminke und Perücke sein zerfallenes Gesicht zu verbergen. Seine Schwester, die Herzogin von Kent, war gestorben, sein Neffe Albert war gestorben, seit 15 Jahren war der Rückgang seines Einflusses sonnenklar. Auch das Europa des Wiener Kongresses, das Europa der kühlen Gleichgewichte war am Absterben. Ein neues Kapitel im großen Buche der Weltgeschichte war eingeleitet.

König Léopold erscheint uns also als eine der letzten Erscheinungen dieses aristokratischen, supernationalen Europas, dem die französische Revolution den ersten Todesstoß gegeben hatte. Industrialisierung, Kapitalismus, bürgerliche Demokratie und nationalistische Leidenschaften wurden jetzt die Schlagwörter einer neuen Epoche, die auch Léopold mit Abscheu vorhergesehen hatte, und die schließlich in den zwei Weltkriegen zum Selbstmord Europas führen sollten.

Für Europa war also Léopold I. 1865 ein abgeschlossenes Kapitel. Aber für Belgien? Wenn man die Geschichte und die Wirkung der Dynastie einigermaßen studiert, so stellt man mit Erstaunen fest, wie sehr die Überlieferung dieses ersten Königs sich bis in unsere Zeit erstreckt hat. Gewiß hatte Léopold für die demokratische Verfassung wenig übrig; dennoch hat er sie peinlichst respektiert, weil er es geschworen hatte und weil diese Verfassung seiner Ansicht nach die Regeln eines Bündnisses zwischen einem Königshaus und einem Volk bestimmten, Regeln die von beiden Parteien geachtet werden mußten. Seinem Sohne Léopold II. hatte er die überseeischen Träume hinterlassen, ohne welche Belgien niemals eine Kolonialmacht geworden wäre. Was König Albert, der 1934 starb und in Belgien als ein Nationalheld gilt, einmal sagte – 'Eigentlich bin ich kein echter Belgier. Ich gehöre zu einer fremden Familie, die mit diesem Volke ein Bündnis geschlossen hat' – das hätte auch Léopold, der Gründer sagen können. Und es ist auch jetzt bekannt, wie König Albert im ersten Weltkriege dieser doppelten Tradition treu geblieben ist: nämlich (1) durch seine Clausewitz'sche, rationelle, unnationale, kühle Interpretierung des Begriffes 'Krieg' und (2) durch seine Auffassung von Belgien, als ein Schlußstein des europäischen Gleichgewichts, auf England von hinten gestützt, deren beide Interessen sich mit dem allgemeinen europäischen Interesse decken, und das daher weder den totalen Sieg des einen noch des anderen wünschen

kann, also mit aller Kraft einen Verständigungsfrieden erstreben
muß. Es ist viel zu früh, um schon jetzt seinen Sohn, Léopold III.,
der 1950 abdanken mußte und heute noch am Leben ist, wissen-
schaftlich studieren zu können. Was man jedoch von ihm weiß,
genügt, um daraus schließen zu können, daß er mit derselben
geistigen und politischen Einstellung einem Adolf Hitler gegenüber stand, wie sein Urahn vor einem Napoleon III. und einem
Bismarck. Die Zeiten sind total anders geworden, Urteile kann
man nur nach vielen Jahrzehnten fällen, in der belgischen Dynastie lebt bis König Baudouin die Überlieferung des ersten Léopold
fort. Sie heißt Frieden, kühles Überlegen, Respekt vor der
Verfassung und hohes Verantwortungsgefühl.

APPENDIX:
PROGRAMME OF THE SEMINAR:
PRINCE ALBERT AND THE
VICTORIAN AGE

22–3 May 1980 in Coburg

Thursday, 22 May 1980

09.00   Welcome address by Dr Klaus Dieter Wolff, President of the
         University of Bayreuth, and The President of the Government of
         Upper Franconia, Wolfgang Winkler.

         Opening of the seminar by His Excellency
         Sir J. Oliver Wright, G.C.V.O., K.C.M.G., D.S.C.,
         Her Majesty's Ambassador to the Federal Republic of Germany
         Venue: Ehrenburg, Riesensaal

09.30   Lecture – Professor Kurt Kluxen, University of Erlangen-Nürnberg:
         'Albert and Europe'

10.45   Lecture – Professor Jacques Willequet, University of Brussels:
         'Leopold I, Victoria's uncle'

12.00   Official welcome of His Royal Highness
         The Duke of Gloucester, G.C.V.O.,
         by Dr Karl Hillermeier, Deputy Minister-President of Bavaria

         Wreath-laying ceremony at The Prince Albert Memorial performed
         by His Royal Highness The Duke of Gloucester, Dr Karl Hillermeier
         and The Lord Mayor of Coburg   *Venue: Market Place*

12.15   Reception in the Guildhall – Continuation of the seminar

14.30   A Message from His Royal Highness The Prince Philip,
         Duke of Edinburgh, Patron of the seminar, conveyed by
         His Royal Highness The Duke of Gloucester
         Venue: Ehrenburg

15.00   Lecture – The Rt. Hon. the Lord Briggs, M.A.,
         Provost of Worcester College, Oxford:
         'Prince Albert and the Arts and Sciences'

Appendix

15.45   Discussion – Chairman: Professor Dr Gertrud Walter,
University of Erlangen-Nürnberg

16.30   Opening of The Prince Albert Exhibition by His Royal Highness
The Duke of Gloucester, with an introduction to the exhibition by
Dr Jürgen Erdmann, Director of the State Library
Venue: Ehrenburg, Silbersaal

19.30   Gala Evening
Carl Maria von Weber 'Der Freischütz' in the Landestheater

Friday, 23 May 1980. Continuation of the seminar

09.00   Lecture
The Rt. Hon. the Lord Blake, M.A., F.B.A., J.P.,
Provost of the Queen's College, Oxford:
'The Prince Consort and Queen Victoria's Prime Ministers'
Venue: Ehrenburg, Sitzungssaal

09.45   Discussion – Chairman: Professor Dr Erwin Wolff,
University of Erlangen-Nürnberg

10.45   Lecture – Sir Robin Mackworth-Young, K.C.V.O., F.S.A.,
Librarian, Windsor Castle:
'Queen Victoria and Prince Albert in Coburg'
Venue: Ehrenburg, Sitzungssaal

11.30   Closing session – Chairman: Professor Dr Thomas Finkenstaedt,
University of Augsburg

13.00   Tree-planting ceremony performed by His Royal Highness
The Duke of Gloucester, in Rosenau Park

13.30   Luncheon – Park Restaurant, Rosenau Castle
Host: Herr Helmut Knauer,
Chairman of the Coburg Rural District Council

15.30   Opportunity to visit Rosenau Castle